QUICK SMART
EASY COOKING IN MINUTES

The pleasure of good eating comes from many things. Good ingredients, enjoyable company, reliable recipes — and, of course, *enough time* to get everything cooked and on to the table.

For many of us time is the element that's hardest to find.

We all seem to be in a constant hurry these days. There's work, children, shopping, keeping the house in order. Often, last of all these priorities, comes the time to cook and enjoy mealtimes together.

What can be done to help? The answer: discover quick and easy ways to cook meals everyone can enjoy. That's where the Quick Smart Cookbook comes in.

Every recipe has been carefully timed to help you. Most clock in at half an hour or less from start to finish, and there's nothing that cannot be prepared in well under 60 minutes. All produce good 'real' food that tastes delicious.

The best thing about this book is that it puts *you* first. The recipes will allow you to fit in all the important things in your life — family, friends and work — and still make it possible for you to bring nice meals to the table. All with minimum fuss and in the shortest possible time.

As so often in the kitchen, it helps to plan ahead. A well-stocked store cupboard is a great help to speed your Quick Smart cooking. Turn to page 48 for useful tips.

Editor Philip Gore **Design** Craig Osment **Art Director** Stephen Joseph **Cookery Editor** Loukie Werle **Food Stylist** Wendy Berecry **Food for Photography** Belinda Clayton **Photography** Warren Webb **Assistant Cookery Editor** Penelope Peel **Editorial Production** Margaret Gore & Associates **Typesetting** APT Pty Ltd **Printed** by Hannanprint, Sydney **Published** by Century Magazines Pty Ltd, 216-224 Commonwealth Street, Surry Hills, NSW 2010, Australia. **UK Distribution** T.B. Clarke (UK) Distributors, Beckett House, 14 Billing Road, Northampton NN1 5AW. Tel: (0604) 23 0941. Fax: (0604) 23 0942. **Australian Distribution** (Supermarkets) Store-Wide Magazine Distributors, Suite 402, 7 Merriwa Street, Gordon, NSW 2072. (Newsagents) NDD 150 Bourke Road, Alexandria, NSW 2015. ©**Century Magazines Pty Ltd** *Recommended retail price. **Photography Credits** We gratefully acknowledge **Mid City Home and Garden** Sydney; **Accoutrement** Mosman; **The Design Store** Spit Junction; **Opus** Paddington; **Corso di Fiori** Chatswood; **Barbara's House and Garden** Birkenhead Point; **Villa Italiana** Mosman; **Pazotti Tiles** Woollahra; **Country Floors** Woollahra; **Australian East India Company** Darlinghurst; **Hale Imports** Brookvale; **Villeroy & Boch** Brookvale; **Country Floors** Woolahra.

SWIFT SOUPS

These soups are quick to make and perfect as a starter or light meal served with crusty bread.

Carrot Soup with Coriander

35 minutes

50g (1¾oz) butter

½ cup spring onions (scallions), chopped

½ cup chopped coriander

4 cups chicken stock

1 tspn cracked black pepper

500g (1lb) carrots, peeled and chopped

1 large potato, peeled and chopped

¼ cup thickened cream

¼ cup chopped parsley

1 Melt the butter in a large saucepan over medium heat. Add the spring onions and coriander and cook for 2 minutes.

2 Add the stock, pepper, carrots and potato and bring to the boil. Reduce heat and simmer for 20 minutes or until vegetables are tender.

3 Puree the vegetables and stock in a blender or food processor until smooth. Return soup to saucepan and heat through.

4 Ladle into warmed soup bowls and top with a spoonful of cream and sprinkle with chopped parsley.

Serves 4

Beggar's Soup

15 minutes

1 French bread stick, cut into thin slices

1 clove garlic, cut in half

4 cups chicken stock

1 cup broccoli

½ cup grated Parmesan cheese

1 Toast the bread on both sides and rub it with the garlic.

2 Bring chicken stock to the boil, add the broccoli and cook for 30 seconds.

3 Ladle soup into warmed soup bowls, place two or three pieces of garlic toast in each bowl and sprinkle with Parmesan cheese.

Serves 4

Carrot Soup with Coriander (top); Beggar's Soup (bottom)

Chicken Soup

6 minutes

8 cups chicken stock

1kg (2lb) finely chopped, cooked chicken

1 clove garlic, peeled, finely chopped

2 tspn Worcestershire sauce

2 cups cream

salt

pepper

4 tblspn chopped fresh parsley

4 tblspn chopped fresh chives

1 Bring stock to a boil. Reduce heat and simmer gently. Add chicken, garlic and Worcestershire sauce. Cook 1-2 minutes to heat through chicken.

2 Add cream, season to taste with salt and freshly ground pepper. Add chopped herbs. Serve immediately.

Serves 8

Green Minestrone

30 minutes

60g (2oz) butter

1 bunch asparagus, chopped, tips reserved

2 cups broccoli tips

½ cup chopped spring onions (scallions)

¾ cup peas

1 cup shelled broad beans

2 chicken stock cubes, crumbled

½ cup peas, extra

1 cup green beans, trimmed

1 Heat the butter in a large saucepan over moderate heat. Add the asparagus stalks, broccoli, spring onions, peas and broad beans, toss in the butter and cook until just softened.

2 Add stock cubes and enough water to cover vegetables, cook until tender.

3 Puree vegetable soup mixture in a blender or food processor until smooth, return puree to saucepan and heat through.

Green Minestrone

4 Add the reserved asparagus tips, extra peas and green beans, and cook for a further 5 minutes. Serve soup with fresh bread rolls.

Serves 4

Mushroom Soup

16 minutes

60g (2oz) unsalted butter

1 onion, roughly chopped

500g (1lb) mushrooms, sliced

4 cups chicken stock

3 egg yolks

salt

pepper

chives, finely chopped

cream

1 Melt butter in a large saucepan. Add onion, cook 2 minutes. Add mushrooms and cook, stirring frequently, for 4 minutes. Add stock, bring to a boil.

2 Puree mushroom mixture in a blender or food processor. Return to saucepan over a low heat.

3 Beat egg yolks together. Beat ½ cup of warm mushroom mixture into yolks. Gradually pour yolk mixture back into remaining soup, stirring constantly. Do not boil.

4 Season soup with salt and freshly ground pepper. Serve hot with chives and a dollop of cream.

Serves 6-8

Tomato and Leek Soup with Mussels (top); Cold Beetroot Soup (bottom)

Tomato and Leek Soup with Mussels

25 minutes

12 mussels, scrubbed and debearded

1 cup dry white wine

2 tblspn olive oil

1 clove garlic, finely chopped

1 leek, white part only, finely sliced

1 cup tinned tomatoes, seeded and chopped

¼ cup tomato puree

2 cups chicken stock

1 tblspn chopped fresh dill

1 Combine mussels and wine in a medium saucepan, bring wine to the boil and cook mussels until their shells open, discard any that don't open. Remove mussels with a slotted spoon and set aside, reserve liquid.

2 Heat the oil in a large deep frying pan, add the garlic and leek and cook for 3 minutes, stirring constantly.

3 Add the tomatoes, puree, stock and reserved liquid, simmer over low heat for 10 minutes. Add the mussels and serve soup in a tureen, sprinkled with dill.

Serves 4

Cold Beetroot Soup

5 minutes — make sure tin of beets and yoghurt are thoroughly chilled

850g (1lb 11oz) tin cooked and peeled baby beets

1 tspn cracked black pepper

¼ cup natural yoghurt

continental parsley for garnish

1 Puree the baby beets and the juice with the pepper in a blender or food processor until smooth. You may need to add a little water if consistency is too thick.

2 Serve with a spoonful of yoghurt on top and parsley sprig.

Serves 4

Gazpacho with Sauteed Scallops

15 minutes — all ingredients should be chilled before starting the soup

7 tomatoes, seeded and chopped

1 clove garlic, peeled, sliced

4 thick slices of Italian bread

½ cup olive oil

4 tblspn red wine vinegar

6 cups chilled tomato juice

2 tblspn chopped fresh basil

1 Spanish onion, peeled, chopped

3 green capsicum (peppers), seeded, chopped

3 tspn Worcestershire sauce

½ tspn Tabasco sauce

salt

pepper

2 cups white wine

juice of ½ lemon

750g (1½lb) scallops

1 Puree tomatoes, garlic and bread roughly in a processor. With motor running, add oil and vinegar. Puree until smooth. Add tomato juice and basil. Refrigerate.

2 Place an onion, capsicum and cucumber in processor, chop coarsely. Add to tomato mixture, together with Worcestershire sauce and Tabasco sauce. Season to taste with salt and freshly ground pepper. Pour soup into individual chilled soup bowls, place in refrigerator to keep cool.

3 Heat wine and lemon juice in a saucepan. Gently poach scallops until opaque, about 2 minutes. Divide between soup bowls and serve immediately.

Serves 6

Watercress Soup

18 minutes

2 bunches watercress

60g (2oz) unsalted butter

1 leek, washed and chopped

1 large potato, peeled and diced

6 cups chicken stock

salt

pepper

pinch of nutmeg

1 cup cream

1 Wash watercress very carefully. Reserve 6 sprigs for garnish. Cut remainder into short lengths.

2 Melt butter, add leek and potato. Saute gently until soft, but not brown. Add stock and simmer 10 minutes. Add watercress, season to taste with salt, freshly ground pepper and nutmeg. Simmer 5 minutes.

3 Puree in a processor or blender. Return to saucepan. Adjust seasoning, add cream and serve with a sprig of watercress for garnish.

Serves 6

Egg Ribbon Soup

8 minutes

¾ cup fresh breadcrumbs

½ cup freshly grated Parmesan cheese

pepper

pinch of nutmeg

3 eggs, lightly beaten

5 cups chicken stock

1 bunch fresh coriander

1 Combine breadcrumbs and Parmesan, freshly ground pepper and nutmeg. Stir in beaten eggs.

2 Bring chicken stock to the boil. Reduce heat to low and slowly add breadcrumb mixture, stirring constantly. Cover, simmer 5 minutes.

3 Stir soup, ladle into bowls and serve immediately with a garnish of coriander leaves.

Serves 6

Winter Vegetable Soup

40 minutes

5 tblspn unsalted butter

4 leeks, washed and sliced

2 cloves garlic, peeled, finely chopped

2 parsnips, peeled, sliced

2 carrots, peeled, sliced

1 large celeriac, peeled, chopped

3 large potatoes, sliced

1 white turnip, peeled, chopped

2 swedes, peeled, chopped

6 cups chicken stock

1 can lima beans, drained

salt

pepper

1 bunch fresh dill

1 Melt butter, slowly cook leeks and garlic for 5 minutes. Do not brown.

2 Add parsnips, carrots, celeriac, potatoes, turnip, swedes and stock. Simmer 20 minutes. Add lima beans and cook another 10 minutes. Puree in a processor or blender until smooth.

3 Return soup to saucepan. Heat through. Add salt and freshly ground pepper to taste. Serve hot, garnished with lots of chopped fresh dill.

Serves 6

French Onion Soup

10 minutes

50g (1¾ oz) butter

4 medium onions, peeled and finely chopped

2 beef stock cubes, crumbled

4 cups water

1 French bread stick, cut into 12 slices

60g (2oz) tasty cheese, grated

3 tblspn brandy

1 Melt the butter in a large saucepan over moderate heat. Add the onions and cook until tender.

2 Add the stock cubes and cook, stirring frequently, for 3 minutes. Add the water and bring to simmering point.

3 Toast the French bread on both sides, top with a small pile of cheese and grill until melted.

4 Stir the brandy into the soup and ladle into serving bowls. Place two or three slices of cheese toast on top of each bowl of soup.

Serves 4

Artichoke and Prawn (Shrimp) Bisque

35 minutes

50g (1¾oz) butter

1 onion, peeled and chopped

2 medium potatoes, peeled and cut into 1cm (½in) dice

1½ cups tinned artichoke hearts, drained

3 cups milk

½ tspn ground paprika

¼ tspn ground black pepper

1 cup school prawns (shrimp), peeled

chives for garnish

1 Melt the butter in a large saucepan, add the onion and potato and cook gently for 5 minutes.

2 Stir in the artichoke hearts, milk, paprika and pepper. Bring soup to the boil, reduce heat and simmer for 20 minutes.

3 Puree the soup in a blender or food processor, return to saucepan and heat gently.

4 Bring to the boil, add prawns, reserving a few for garnish and ladle into soup bowls. Garnish with chopped chives and prawns.

Serves 4

French Onion Soup (top); Artichoke and Prawn (Shrimp) Bisque (bottom)

APPETISING STARTERS

When you're in a hurry, these tasty first courses will provide the perfect start to your meal.

Taramasalata

40 minutes — includes chilling time

50g (1¾oz) crustless white bread

¾ cup milk

1 onion, peeled and grated

1 clove garlic, crushed

¼ cup freshly squeezed lemon juice

¼ cup red caviar

¼ cup olive oil

1 Soak the bread in the milk for 5 minutes.

2 In a blender or food processor, puree the bread and milk with the onion, garlic, lemon juice and caviar, until mixture is smooth.

3 While motor is running, gradually add the oil, drop by drop. Chill for 30 minutes before serving, and serve with bread, toast or plain biscuits.

Serves 4

Curly Endive Salad with Hot Pancetta Dressing

8 minutes

4 cups curly endive

2 slices rolled pancetta, 1cm (½in) thick

¼ cup raspberry vinegar

¼ cup olive oil

salt

pepper

Avocado with Caviar (top);
Taramasalata (bottom)

1 Place curly endive in a salad bowl.

2 Cut pancetta into 1cm (½in) cubes. Saute in a very hot frying pan until golden brown on all sides. Add vinegar to frying pan, allow to come to a boil.

3 Remove pan from heat, whisk in oil. Season to taste with salt and freshly ground pepper.

4 Pour dressing over curly endive while still hot, toss well. Serve immediately.

Serves 4

Avocado with Caviar

15 minutes

2 ripe avocados

2 tblspn freshly squeezed lemon juice

200g (6½oz) cream cheese

3 tblspn mayonnaise

1 tblspn freshly squeezed lemon juice, extra

¼ tspn ground nutmeg

2 tblspn caviar for garnish

1 Cut each avocado in half, remove stone and lightly brush flesh with lemon juice.

2 Using a blender, food processor or electric mixer, mix the cream cheese with the mayonnaise, extra lemon juice and nutmeg, until smooth.

3 Divide mixture between each avocado half, and fill the cavity. Sprinkle caviar over the top and serve immediately.

Serves 4

Marinated Baked Goat's Cheese

45 minutes — includes marinating time

⅔ cup olive oil

1 tblspn fresh thyme, chopped

1 clove garlic, crushed

¼ tspn cracked black pepper

400g (13oz) Chevre or other goat's cheese, cut into 4 slices

1 cup dried breadcrumbs

½ red capsicum (pepper), seeded, cut into very fine strips

toast

1 In a small flat dish, combine the olive oil, thyme, garlic and pepper. Add the slices of cheese, cover and marinate for 30 minutes.

2 Remove the cheese from marinade and coat in breadcrumbs. Place the cheese in a baking dish and cook in a moderate oven for 10 minutes. Remove from oven and leave for 3 minutes before serving.

3 Place each cheese slice on serving plate and garnish with the watercress and capsicum, serve with toast.

Serves 4

Mozzarella Tomato Salad (top); Marinated Baked Goat's Cheese (bottom)

Mozzarella Tomato Salad

5 minutes

4 ripe tomatoes, sliced

200g (6½oz) mozzarella cheese, sliced

fresh basil leaves

⅔ cup olive oil

3 tblspn red wine vinegar

¼ tspn cracked black pepper

2 tspn finely chopped basil

1 tblspn thickened cream

1 Arrange the tomato slices and cheese on a serving plate. Garnish with basil leaves.

2 Dress with combined olive oil, red wine vinegar, pepper, chopped basil and thickened cream.

Serves 4

Salad of Warm Asparagus and Quail's Eggs

15 minutes

4 cups mixed salad greens

⅓ cup roughly chopped combined basil and parsley

½ cup vinaigrette

24 asparagus spears, trimmed

2 tblspn unsalted butter

16 quail's eggs

pepper

sprigs of parsley and basil for garnish

1 In a large bowl combine greens with herbs. Toss with vinaigrette, arrange on 4 plates.

2 Steam asparagus until tender, but not limp, about 3-4 minutes. Remove to a double thickness tea-towel to drain.

3 Melt butter in a large frying pan, crack quail's eggs gently, fry until just set.

4 Place asparagus on salad, top with 4 fried quail's eggs each. Sprinkle with freshly ground black pepper. Serve warm, garnished with sprigs of herbs.

Serves 4

Antipasto Salad

Smoked Salmon Pate

5 minutes

125g (4oz) smoked salmon

125g (4oz) cottage cheese

250g (½lb) unsalted butter

1 tblspn dry sherry

1 tblspn mayonnaise

1 tblspn freshly squeezed lemon juice

pepper

Tabasco sauce

1 Blend salmon and cottage cheese in a processor. Melt butter over a very low heat and, with machine running, add to salmon mixture.

2 Add sherry, mayonnaise and lemon juice, process 30 seconds. Season to taste with freshly ground pepper and Tabasco sauce.

3 Serve at room temperature with toast or crackers.

Serves 4-6

Red Capsicum (Pepper) Marinated in Garlic and Oil

45 minutes — includes marinating time

4 large red capsicum (peppers)

¼ cup olive oil

1 clove garlic, slivered

salt

pepper

toasted slices of French bread to scrvc

1 Char capsicum over a gas flame or under a grill until black and blistery all over. Place in a paper bag, seal, leave to sweat for 10 minutes.

2 Rub off skin, remove seeds, rinse quickly under cold running water, dry with paper towels.

3 Chop roughly into 1cm (½in) pieces, place in a serving bowl. Add oil and garlic, toss well. Season to taste with salt and freshly ground pepper.

4 Stand at room temperature for 20 minutes. Serve with toasted slices of French bread.

Serves 4-6

Antipasto Salad

40 minutes — includes marinating time

1 cup cauliflowerets

¼ cup sun-dried tomatoes

12 large rounds of salami, cut into strips

½ cup mozzarella cheese, cut into 1cm (½in) cubes

10 stuffed olives, cut in halves

2 zucchini (courgette), cut into thin 5cm (2in) lengths

DRESSING

½ cup olive oil

3 tblspn vinegar

3 tblspn freshly squeezed lemon juice

½ tspn cracked black pepper

2 cloves garlic, crushed

½ cup basil leaves

1 Place the cauliflower, sun-dried tomatoes, salami, cheese, olives and zucchini in a medium bowl.

2 Add the olive oil, vinegar, lemon juice, pepper and garlic and mix well. Cover and marinate at room temperature for 30 minutes.

3 Arrange salad on serving plates, pour over a little of the marinade and garnish with fresh basil leaves.

Serves 4

Potato Patties with Smoked Trout

30 minutes

3 potatoes, peeled and grated

1 large onion, peeled and grated

2 eggs, lightly beaten

2 tblspn plain flour

½ tspn cracked black pepper

2 tblspn butter

8 slices smoked trout

¼ cup sour cream

watercress for garnish

1 Squeeze excess water from potatoes and onions and mix with the eggs, flour and pepper.

2 Melt the butter in a large frying pan over moderate heat. Add the potato batter in 1-2 tablespoon batches, leaving 2cm (¾in) of space between each one. Cook until patties are golden, about 5 minutes per side; drain on paper towels.

3 Arrange trout on each serving plate, place two patties on each plate and garnish with sour cream and watercress.

Serves 4

Poached Egg with Vinaigrette Dressing

10 minutes

4 eggs

1 lettuce, washed

¼ cup finely chopped bacon, fried

4 tblspn red wine vinegar

2 tblspn olive oil

¼ tspn cracked black pepper

2 tblspn red wine

1 Bring a shallow frying pan of water to the boil. Reduce heat to a simmer, add eggs, one at a time, and poach until whites are set.

Poached Egg with Vinaigrette Dressing (top); Potato Patties with Smoked Trout (bottom)

2 Arrange a bed of lettuce on each entree plate, top with a poached egg and sprinkle with bacon.

3 Just before serving pour over combined red wine vinegar, oil, pepper and red wine. Serve immediately.

Serves 4

Kipper Pate

8 minutes

250g (½lb) kipper fillets

1 onion

1 French bread, cut into diagonal slices

½ cup mayonnaise

salt

pepper

parsley for garnish

1 Place kipper fillets in a bowl, pour over boiling water to cover. Stand 5 minutes.

2 Meanwhile, chop onion and toast bread slices.

3 Drain kippers, flake fish into a dry bowl. Remove any bones. Add onion and mayonnaise, season to taste with salt and freshly ground pepper. Mix well. Sprinkle top with parsley.

4 Serve with toasted French bread slices.

Serves 4

Crostini with Provolone and Salami

10 minutes

1 baguette, diagonally cut into 1cm (½in) slices

olive oil

2 large cloves garlic, halved

pepper

12 slices salami

12 slices provolone, roughly same size as bread

parsley for garnish

1 Grill baguette slices on one side until golden brown. Remove from grill, brush other side with oil, rub with cut side of garlic.

2 Sprinkle liberally with freshly ground pepper. Grill this side until golden.

3 Place a slice of salami on oiled side of bread, followed by cheese. Return to grill until cheese has melted.

4 Serve hot, garnished with parsley.

Serves 4

Spanish Onion and Bacon Pizzas

20 minutes

500g (1lb) rindless bacon, cut into 5cm (2in) pieces

6 pita breads, 15cm (6in) diameter

2 tblspn olive oil

¼ cup finely chopped fresh basil

¼ tspn chilli flakes

2 tomatoes, thinly sliced

1 Spanish onion, sliced, rings separated

185g (6oz) grated mozzarella

1 Fry bacon in a frying pan until crispy, about 6 minutes. Drain on paper towels.

2 Place pitas on a baking sheet, brush with oil, sprinkle with basil and chilli flakes.

3 Divide tomatoes, onion rings and bacon among pitas, top with grated cheese.

4 Bake in the centre of a 230°C (450°F) oven until cheese is bubbly, about 8 minutes. Cut into wedges, serve hot.

Serves 4-6

Satisfying Salads

Crisp and fresh, these salads are easy to prepare and full of goodness.

Chicken and Pineapple Salad with Curry Dressing

5 minutes

2 cups watercress sprigs

1 cooked chicken, skin removed, meat torn into pieces

1 cup pineapple pieces, drained

½ cup walnut halves

½ cup cherry tomatoes, cut in halves

¼ cup French dressing

2 tspn mild curry powder

1 Arrange the watercress, chicken pieces, pineapple, walnuts and tomatoes on serving plate.

2 Pour over combined French dressing and curry powder.

Serves 4

Left-over Rare Beef and Potato Salad

10 minutes

2 cups minced rare roast beef

2 cups sliced cooked potatoes

1 cup crunchy cooked French beans, cut into 2cm (¾in) pieces

1 cup sliced radish

1 cup pecan nuts, roughly chopped

¾ cup egg mayonnaise

¼ cup chopped parsley

1 Combine beef, potatoes, beans, radish and nuts in a salad bowl. Toss gently.

2 Add mayonnaise, toss again, until whole salad is well coated. Serve immediately sprinkled with parsley.

Serves 4

Tofu and Broccoli Salad with Peanut Sauce

15 minutes

2½ cups broccoli flowerets

200g (6½oz) tofu, cut into 2cm (¾in) cubes

1 red capsicum (pepper), seeded and cut into 1cm (½in) squares

3 tblspn smooth peanut butter

½ cup cream

1 Bring a large saucepan of water to the boil, add broccoli and cook for 1 minute. Remove broccoli with a slotted spoon and refresh under cold water. Arrange broccoli, tofu and capsicum on serving plate.

2 Heat the peanut butter in a medium saucepan over low heat. Stir in half the cream until combined.

3 Remove from heat, stir in remainder of cream and 3 tablespoons of water. Pour sauce over salad and serve immediately.

Serves 4

Chicken and Pineapple Salad with Curry Dressing (top); Tofu and Broccoli Salad with Peanut Sauce (bottom)

Witlof (Chicory, Belgian Endive) Salad with Pan-fried Gypsy Ham

10 minutes

1 tblspn unsalted butter

8 slices gypsy ham, each 0.5cm (¼in) thick

2 heads witlof (UK chicory, US Belgian endive), leaves separated

DRESSING

⅓ cup chopped parsley

1 tblspn freshly squeezed lemon juice

2 tblspn walnut oil

salt

pepper

1 To make dressing: Combine parsley, lemon juice and oil in a screwtop jar, shake until well combined. Season to taste with salt and freshly ground pepper.

2 Melt butter in a large frying pan over moderate heat. Add half the ham slices, brown on both sides, about 3 minutes, turning once. Remove from pan, keep warm. Repeat procedure with remaining ham slices.

3 Place witlof on one side of four plates, arrange ham on other side. Pour dressing over witlof, serve immediately.

Serves 4

Warm Salad with Italian Sausages

20 minutes

8 cups mixed salad greens, torn into bite-size pieces

1 tspn olive oil

8 hot Italian sausages

6 spring onions (scallions), sliced

½ cup red wine vinegar

2 tblspn olive oil, extra

2 tspn Dijon mustard

salt

pepper

1 Arrange salad greens in a large bowl.

2 Heat olive oil in a large frying pan. Add sausages, cook over medium heat until golden brown all over and cooked through.

3 Remove sausages from pan with a slotted spoon, drain on paper towels. Cut into 1cm (½in) slices.

4 Reheat fat in frying pan. Add spring onions, saute 1 minute. Add vinegar, bring to a boil, scraping up any browned bits from the bottom.

5 Whisk in oil and mustard, add sausages. Toss to coat. Season to taste with salt and freshly ground pepper. Pour contents of pan over salad greens, toss well. Serve immediately.

Serves 4

Avocado, Grapefruit and Pawpaw (Papaya) Salad with Prawns (Shrimp)

20 minutes

8 cups mixed salad greens, torn into bite-size pieces

1 large avocado, halved, stoned, peeled, cut into chunks

1 large grapefruit, peeled, pith removed, segmented

1 medium pawpaw (papaya), halved, seeded, peeled, cut into chunks

24 cooked prawns (shrimp), shelled and deveined, tails intact

DRESSING

⅓ cup white wine vinegar

1 egg yolk, beaten

1 clove garlic, crushed

½ cup olive oil

1 tblspn chopped fresh chives

salt

1 To make dressing: Combine vinegar, egg yolk, garlic, oil and chives in a screwtop jar. Shake until well combined. Season to taste with salt.

2 Add enough dressing to salad greens to coat lightly. Arrange greens in the centre of 4 plates.

3 Arrange avocado, grapefruit, pawpaw and prawns on top and around greens. Drizzle with a little more dressing, pass remaining dressing separately. Serve immediately.

Serves 4

Salad Nicoise

10 minutes

1½ cups beans, trimmed

1 cup tinned tuna, drained and broken into bite-size pieces

½ cup cherry tomatoes, quartered

4 hard-boiled eggs, sliced

12 black olives

8 tinned anchovy fillets, drained

1 tblspn chopped chives

1 tblspn drained capers

2 tblspn olive oil

2 tblspn French dressing

1 clove garlic, crushed

1 Bring a medium saucepan of water to the boil over moderate heat. Add the beans and cook for 1 minute, drain. Refresh under cold water, drain again and set aside.

2 Arrange beans, tuna, tomatoes, egg slices, olives and anchovy fillets on a serving plate.

3 Sprinkle with chives and capers and dress with combined olive oil, French dressing and crushed garlic.

Serves 4

Salad Nicoise

Smoked Beef and Artichoke Salad

7 minutes

8 slices cold smoked beef

1 cup alfalfa sprouts

½ cup artichoke hearts, drained, halved

¼ red capsicum (pepper), seeded, cut into thin strips

4 tblspn olive oil

3 tblspn red wine vinegar

¼ tspn cracked black pepper

1 tspn chopped parsley

1 Roll up each slice of beef and arrange decoratively on a bed of alfalfa. Place artichoke halves between each roll and garnish with capsicum strips.

2 Dress salad with combined oil, red wine vinegar, cracked pepper and chopped parsley.

Serves 4

Chinese Salad with Crab and Snowpeas

15 minutes

2 cups snowpeas, topped and tailed

1 cup thinly sliced carrots

500g (1lb) chow mein noodles

500g (½lb) crabmeat, flaked

1 cucumber, peeled, seeded, thinly sliced

⅓ cup chopped spring onions (scallions)

DRESSING

¼ cup olive oil

¼ cup freshly squeezed lemon juice

¼ cup chopped fresh coriander

salt

pepper

1 To make dressing: Combine oil, lemon juice and coriander in a screwtop jar. Shake until well combined. Season to taste with salt and freshly ground pepper.

2 In a large saucepan, bring very lightly salted water to the boil. Add snowpeas and carrots, cook 1 minute. Remove with a slotted spoon, refresh under cold running water. Pat dry with paper towels.

3 Add noodles to boiling water, cook 1 minute, drain. Rinse under cold running water, drain thoroughly. Place in a salad bowl.

4 Add snowpeas and carrots to bowl, then flaked crab, cucumber and spring onions. Pour over dressing, toss well to coat. Serve immediately or refrigerate until chilled.

Serves 4-6

Sauteed Tuna Salad with Garlic and Anchovy Dressing

10 minutes

cos lettuce leaves

750g (1½lb) tuna (mackerel, halibut) steaks, cut into 2.5cm (1in) cubes

2 tblspn olive oil

lemon wedges to garnish

DRESSING

⅓ cup virgin olive oil

¼ cup chopped fresh parsley

2 tblspn freshly squeezed lemon juice

1 tspn anchovy paste

2 cloves garlic, crushed

salt

pepper

1 Line a platter with lettuce leaves.

2 To make dressing: Combine oil, parsley, lemon juice, anchovy paste and garlic in a screwtop jar. Shake until well combined. Season to taste with salt and freshly ground pepper.

3 Saute tuna in a frying pan in hot oil until golden brown on the outside, still pink inside.

4 Arrange tuna on top of lettuce, drizzle with dressing, garnish with lemon wedges. Serve immediately.

Serves 4

Smoked Beef and Artichoke Salad

Tomato, Corn and Prawn (Shrimp) Salad

10 minutes

2 cups cooked corn kernels

1 onion, finely chopped

1 cup shelled, deveined cooked prawns (shrimp), cut into 1cm (½in) lengths

2 tomatoes, chopped

¼ cup spring onions (scallions), chopped

1 red capsicum (pepper), seeded and finely chopped

2 tblspn red wine vinegar

2 tblspn olive oil

1 clove garlic, crushed

1 tblspn freshly squeezed lemon juice

1 In a large bowl, combine the corn, onion, prawns, tomato, spring onions and capsicum, mix well.

2 Mix together the vinegar, oil, garlic and lemon juice and toss through the salad.

Serves 4

Prawn (Shrimp) and Snowpea Salad with Sweet Chilli Sauce

15 minutes

¾ cup sweet white wine

1 tblspn freshly squeezed lemon juice

1 tblspn freshly squeezed lime juice

1 tspn sugar

1 tspn sambal oelek (chilli paste)

1 tspn cracked black pepper

½ tspn ground coriander

315g (10oz) scallops, deveined

315g (10oz) king prawns (shrimp), deveined, peeled, tails intact

75g (2½oz) snowpeas

2 tblspn oil

1 tblspn chopped parsley

1 Heat the wine, lemon juice, lime juice, sugar, chilli paste, pepper and coriander in a large frying pan over moderate heat, until boiling.

Prawn (Shrimp) and Snowpea Salad with Sweet Chilli Sauce

2 Reduce heat, simmer, add scallops and prawns, cook for 2 minutes or until cooked through. Remove with a slotted spoon and set aside.

3 Add snowpeas to the frying pan, cook for 30 seconds, remove with slotted spoon and add to the prawns and scallops.

4 Add the oil and parsley to the pan juices, cook for 1 minute, then pour over the scallops, prawns and snowpeas. Toss well and chill until ready to serve.

Serves 4

Fish Salad with Green Aioli

10 minutes

3 tblspn butter

1 clove garlic, crushed

440g (14oz) bream (sea perch, pompano) fillet, cut into 2cm (¾in) squares

2 cups watercress sprigs

Fish Salad with Green Aioli (top); Tomato, Corn and Prawn (Shrimp) Salad (bottom)

GREEN AIOLI

3 egg yolks

½ cup chopped parsley

½ cup chopped basil

¼ cup chopped chives

2 tblspn freshly squeezed lemon juice

1 clove garlic, crushed

1 cup oil

1 Melt the butter in a large frying pan over moderate heat, add the garlic, cook for 1 minute.

2 Add fish pieces and cook for 2 minutes each side or until cooked through.

3 Meanwhile, to make mayonnaise: Place the egg yolks, parsley, basil and chives, lemon juice and extra garlic in a blender or food processor. While motor is operating, gradually add the oil, drop by drop until mayonnaise is of a suitable consistency.

4 Arrange the watercress and fish pieces on a serving plate, pour mayonnaise over the top.

Serves 4

Chicken Salad with Parmesan Cheese and Tomatoes

25 minutes

4 chicken fillets

2 tblspn olive oil

1 tblspn chopped continental parsley

1 clove garlic, crushed

salt

pepper

1 lettuce, torn into bite-size pieces

1/3 cup coarse Parmesan cheese shavings

12 cherry tomatoes, halved

DRESSING

1 tspn anchovy paste

1 clove garlic, crushed

juice of 1 lemon

1 tblspn white wine vinegar

1/2 cup virgin olive oil

1 egg yolk, beaten

salt

pepper

1 Place chicken fillets in a bowl. Combine oil, parsley and garlic in a screwtop jar, shake until well combined. Season to taste with salt and freshly ground pepper. Pour over chicken, turn fillets several times to coat thoroughly. Stand at room temperature for 10 minutes.

2 Meanwhile, make dressing: Combine anchovy paste, garlic, lemon juice, vinegar, oil and egg yolk in a screwtop jar. Shake until well combined. Season to taste with salt and freshly ground pepper.

3 Place lettuce, cheese and tomato in a salad bowl.

4 Heat a heavy non-stick frying pan over high heat. Fry chicken fillets until tender, about 6 minutes, turning once. Allow to cool slightly, cut into 1cm (1/2in) wide strips.

5 Arrange chicken strips on salad, pour over dressing, toss gently. Serve immediately.

Serves 4

Honey Pork with Julienne Vegetables

30 minutes

350g (11oz) pork fillet

4 tblspn honey

1/4 cup Worcestershire sauce

1 tblspn butter

2 zucchini (courgette), cut into thin strips

1 cucumber, cut into thin strips

1 red capsicum (pepper), cut into thin strips

1 tspn sesame seeds

watercress for garnish

1 Cut pork fillet into thin strips and allow to marinate in combined honey and Worcestershire sauce for 15 minutes.

2 Heat butter in a medium frying pan over moderate heat. Add the marinade and reserve the pork. Cook the marinade until sauce becomes thick, add reserved pork strips and toss in the sauce, cook for about 3 minutes or until cooked through.

3 Arrange the zucchini, cucumber and capsicum strips on a serving plate, top with the pork fillets and sprinkle with sesame seeds. Garnish with fresh watercress.

Serves 4

Honey Pork with Julienne Vegetables

SPEEDY SEAFOOD

These succulent seafood dishes can be prepared in no time at all and are guaranteed to please

Fillet of Bream with White Sauce and Grapes

15 minutes

4 tblspn butter

4 bream (ocean perch, orange roughy) fillets, 200g (6½oz) each

½ cup sliced button mushrooms

24 seedless grapes

½ cup sour cream

¼ cup mayonnaise

1 Melt the butter in a medium frying pan over moderate heat. Add the fish fillets and cook for 3 minutes each side or until just cooked, remove from frying pan and keep warm in a low oven.

2 Add the mushrooms to the frying pan and saute over medium heat for 1 minute. Add the grapes, sour cream and mayonnaise, mix well and cook until just heated through. Serve over fish fillets.

Serves 4

Swordfish with Coriander and Avocado Sauce

15 minutes

4 swordfish steaks, 2.5cm (1in) thick

⅓ cup unsalted butter, melted

salt

pepper

SAUCE

¼ cup olive oil

2 tblspn freshly squeezed lemon juice

⅓ cup chopped spring onions (scallions)

1 clove garlic, crushed

2 tblspn chopped fresh coriander

1 ripe avocado, cut into 0.5cm (¼in) cubes

salt

Tabasco sauce

1 To make sauce: Combine oil, lemon juice, spring onions, garlic, coriander and avocado in a bowl. Season to taste with salt and Tabasco. Stir well. Allow to stand at room temperature.

2 Pre-heat griller. Arrange swordfish on a lightly buttered griller tray, brush fish with butter, season to taste with salt and freshly ground pepper.

3 Grill until golden brown, about 4 minutes. Turn over, brush with butter, grill a further 3-4 minutes, or until fish is cooked through. Serve immediately with coriander and avocado sauce.

Serves 4

Fillet of Bream with White Sauce and Grapes

Salmon Cutlet with Orange Butter

Salmon Cutlet with Orange Butter

15 minutes

125g (4oz) butter, softened

1 tblspn orange juice concentrate

1 tblspn finely grated orange rind

2 tspn finely chopped parsley

3 tblspn butter, extra

4 salmon cutlets, 150g (5oz) each

1 To make orange butter: Combine the butter, orange juice, rind and parsley, mix well and set aside at room temperature.

2 Melt the extra butter in a medium frying pan over moderate heat. Add the salmon cutlets and cook for 3 minutes each side or until cooked through.

3 Place a cutlet on each plate, top with a tablespoon of the orange butter and serve immediately.

Serves 4

Whiting Fillets with Gingered Carrot Sauce

40 minutes

⅓ cup flour

2 whiting (halibut) fillets

1 tblspn freshly squeezed lemon juice

3 tblspn unsalted butter

SAUCE

1 onion, finely chopped

410g (13oz) carrots, peeled, chopped

1 tblspn ground ginger

¾ cup freshly squeezed orange juice

salt

pepper

1 To make sauce: Combine onion, carrot, half the ginger and the orange juice in a saucepan. Add salt and freshly ground pepper to taste. Bring to a boil, reduce heat, cook gently until carrots are tender. Place in a processor, puree. Season to taste with remaining ginger and salt and freshly ground pepper. Keep warm.

2 Meanwhile, place flour in a deep plate. Pat fish dry with paper towels, season with salt and a little of the ginger. Sprinkle with lemon juice. Place fish in flour, coating on both sides, shaking off excess.

3 Heat butter in a non-stick frying pan, add whiting and cook until golden on both sides and fish flakes easily when tested.

4 Place cooked fillets on heated plates, pour carrot sauce over. Serve immediately.

Serves 4

Scallops with Chilli Lime Dressing

Scallops with Chilli Lime Dressing

15 minutes

200g (6½oz) green beans, topped and tailed

200g (6½oz) snowpeas, topped and tailed

1 tblspn butter

¼ cup dry white wine

500g (1lb) scallops, deveined

DRESSING

3 tblspn olive oil

2 tblspn freshly squeezed lime juice

2 tblspn red wine vinegar

1 tspn sambal oelek (chilli paste)

1 tblspn chopped dill

freshly ground pepper

1 Bring a small saucepan of water to the boil, add the beans, cook for 1 minute, then add the snowpeas, cook for 30 seconds, refresh snowpeas and beans under cold water and drain.

2 Melt the butter in a medium saucepan over moderate heat, add the wine and scallops, cook for 3 minutes or until cooked through. Remove with a slotted spoon and set aside.

3 To make dressing: Mix together the oil, lime juice, vinegar, chilli paste, dill and pepper to taste.

4 Arrange beans, snowpeas and scallops on a serving plate. Pour over dressing and serve.

Serves 4

Tuna with Mustard and Mint Sauce

20 minutes

2 tblspn softened unsalted butter

8 tuna (mackerel, yellowtail) steaks, 90g (3oz) each

SAUCE

2 tblspn white wine vinegar

2 tblspn Dijon mustard

½ cup peanut oil

⅓ cup fresh mint leaves

salt

pepper

1 To make sauce: Combine vinegar, mustard, oil and mint in a screwtop jar. Shake until well combined. Season to taste with salt and freshly ground pepper. Allow to stand at room temperature while cooking fish.

2 Brush inside of an ovenproof dish, large enough to hold fish without overlapping, with softened butter. Arrange fish in dish, bake on a low shelf in a 200°C (400°F) oven until just done, about 10 minutes.

3 Transfer tuna to heated plates, pour sauce over fish. Serve immediately.

Serves 4

Baked Fish and Tomato Gratin

35-40 minutes

1 tblspn butter, melted

750g (1½lb) white, boneless fish fillets

2 cups grated mature cheese

4 tomatoes, sliced

1 tblspn finely chopped oregano

2 cloves garlic, crushed

1 Grease an ovenproof baking dish with the butter. Arrange a single layer of fish in the dish. Sprinkle with one third of the cheese and top with half the tomatoes. Dust with oregano, garlic and seasoning.

2 Arrange another layer of fish, cheese and tomato, and finally sprinkle top with the remaining third of the cheese.

3 Bake in a moderate oven for 30 minutes, serve immediately.

Serves 4

Gemfish with Tomato and Basil Sauce

20 minutes

4 gemfish (sea bream, orange roughy) fillets

olive oil

freshly squeezed lemon juice

salt

pepper

SAUCE

375g (¾lb) tomatoes, chopped

4 black olives, stoned, cut into thin slices

⅓ cup chopped fresh basil

2 tblspn chopped fresh chives

¼ cup olive oil

1 tblspn red wine vinegar

salt

pepper

1 To make sauce: Combine tomatoes, olives, basil, chives, oil and vinegar in a bowl, stir well to mix. Season to taste with salt and freshly ground pepper. Allow to stand at room temperature.

2 Brush fillets with oil and lemon juice, season with salt and freshly ground pepper. Place under a pre-heated griller and cook until fish is opaque, about 8 minutes, turning once.

3 Serve on heated plates, spoon sauce over.

Serves 4

Fish with Pistachio Brandy Sauce

20 minutes

4 tblspn butter

4 fish fillets, 200g (6½oz) each

4 tblspn brandy

⅔ cup sour cream

⅔ cup cream

3 tblspn freshly squeezed orange juice

4 tblspn chopped roasted shelled pistachio nuts

very fine strips orange rind for garnish

1 Heat the butter in a large frying pan over moderate heat. Add the fish fillets and cook 3 minutes each side or until just cooked. Set aside in a warm oven.

2 Add the brandy, sour cream, cream and orange juice to the frying pan, cook until sauce is reduced by half.

3 Spoon sauce over fish fillets, sprinkle pistachio nuts on top of sauce and garnish with thin strips of orange rind.

Serves 4

Baked Trout with Dill Sauce

30 minutes

3 tblspn unsalted butter, room temperature

1 clove garlic, crushed

4 trout, 250g (½lb) each

1 lemon, thinly cut into 8 slices

4 spring onions (scallions)

4 dill sprigs

1 tblspn freshly squeezed lemon juice

SAUCE

1 cup sour cream

¼ cup finely chopped fresh dill

1 tspn freshly squeezed lemon juice

salt

pepper

1 To make sauce: Combine sour cream, dill and lemon juice in a bowl, stir until smooth. Season to taste with salt and freshly ground pepper. Allow to stand at room temperature.

2 Butter the inside of an ovenproof dish, large enough to hold fish in a single layer, with 1 tablespoon of the butter.

3 Combine remaining butter with the garlic, use to brush inside of fish. Place 2 lemon slices, a spring onion and dill sprig inside each fish.

4 Place fish side by side in the buttered dish, sprinkle with lemon juice. Cover with foil, bake in a 180°C (350°F) oven until fish is cooked through, about 15-20 minutes.

5 Remove lemon, spring onions and dill sprigs from cavities, serve immediately with sauce.

Serves 4

Baked Fish and Tomato Gratin (top); Fish with Pistachio Brandy Sauce (bottom)

Sweet Soy Octopus

10 minutes

1kg (2lb) baby octopus

3 tblspn honey

2 tblspn butter

3 tblspn Worcestershire sauce

2 cloves garlic, crushed

1 tblspn tomato paste

¼ cup soy sauce

2 tblspn water

1 tblspn finely chopped chives

1 Discard heads and beaks of octopus, rinse and drain.

2 Add the honey and butter to a large frying pan and cook over moderate heat. Add the Worcestershire sauce, garlic, tomato paste, soy sauce and water. Bring to the boil, reduce heat and simmer for 1 minute or until thickened.

3 Add the prepared octopus and cook for 2 minutes or until just cooked.

4 Toss well in the sweet soy sauce and serve immediately, sprinkled with chopped chives.

Serves 4

Seafood Kebabs

25 minutes

16 snowpeas, trimmed

¼ cup butter, melted

3 tblspn freshly squeezed lime juice

1 tblspn finely chopped mint

2 tblspn finely grated Parmesan cheese

16 green king prawns (shrimp), peeled and deveined, tails intact

8 wooden skewers, soaked in water for 10 minutes

16 green scallops, deveined

1 Bring a medium saucepan of water to the boil, add snowpeas, cook for 30 seconds, refresh under cold water, set aside.

2 Combine the butter, lime juice, mint and Parmesan cheese in a small bowl.

Seafood Kebabs (left); Sweet Soy Octopus (above)

3 Thread a prawn onto each skewer, then wrap a scallop in a blanched snowpea and thread onto skewer, add another prawn and snowpea wrapped scallop.

4 Brush each kebab with the butter dressing and grill under a moderate griller, 2 minutes each side, basting regularly. Serve immediately.

Serves 4

Paupiettes of Sole with Prosciutto and Peach in Cheese Sauce

30 minutes

4 sole (Dover sole, flounder)

salt

pepper

4 spring onions (scallions), cut into 5cm (2in) julienne

2 peaches, cut into 5cm (2in) julienne

4 slices prosciutto, cut into 5cm (2in) julienne

parsley for garnish

SAUCE

¾ cup cream

90g (3oz) blue vein cheese

1 To make sauce: Combine cream and cheese in a small saucepan, heat gently until cheese has melted and sauce is smooth. Keep warm.

2 Spread sole fillets on a flat surface. Pat dry with paper towels, season to taste with salt and freshly ground pepper.

3 Place spring onions, peach and prosciutto strips neatly on the fillets, roll up and place in an ovenproof dish, side by side. Pour cheese sauce over, cover dish with foil.

4 Bake in a 180°C (350°F) oven until fish is cooked through, about 20 minutes. Serve immediately.

Serves 4

EGGS AND CHEESE

The versatility of eggs and cheese make them ideal for meals that are both nutritious and easy to make.

Smoked Cod and Blue Cheese Frittata

40 minutes

6 eggs, lightly beaten

1 cup cream

½ cup crumbled blue cheese

1 red capsicum (pepper), seeded and finely chopped

1 tblspn finely chopped chives

2 tblspn finely chopped dill

250g (½lb) smoked cod (smoked haddock), skin removed, cut into 1cm (½in) cubes

1 Combine eggs, cream and blue cheese in a large bowl, mix until well combined. Stir in capsicum, chives, dill and smoked cod, mix well.

2 Pour mixture into a greased, ovenproof 23cm (9in) flan dish and bake in a moderate oven for 30 minutes.

Serves 4

Spanish Omelette

15 minutes

3 tblspn olive oil

3 tblspn unsalted butter

1 cup mixed, diced potatoes, Spanish onion, red and green capsicum (pepper)

2 cloves garlic, finely chopped

3 tblspn peas

8 eggs

salt

pepper

1 Put half the oil and butter in a heavy iron frying pan. Add potatoes, onion, red and green capsicum and garlic. Cook gently, covered, until nearly tender. Add remaining oil, butter and the peas.

2 Beat eggs, pour over vegetables in pan. Stir to mix well, cover, leave to cook gently until set.

3 Divide into 4 wedges and serve immediately.

Serves 4

Chilli Eggs Vinaigrette

10-15 minutes

10 hard-boiled eggs, peeled and cut in half

2 celery stalks, finely sliced

2 tblspn finely chopped spring onions (scallions)

10 stuffed green olives, sliced

3 tblspn olive oil

2 tblspn red wine vinegar

¼ tspn sambal oelek (chilli paste)

1 Arrange eggs, yolk side up, in a serving bowl. Arrange celery, spring onions and olives on top and dress with combined vinegar, oil and sambal oelek.

Serves 4

Smoked Cod and Blue Cheese Frittata (top); Chilli Eggs Vinaigrette (bottom)

Herb a...
Souffle...

40 minute...

50g (1¾oz,...

3 tblspn pl...

300ml (½p...

155g (5oz)...

75g (2½oz...

¼ tspn gr...

1 cup cho...

4 eggs, se...

1 Mel...
   sau...
Add the...
slowly...
constar...
smooth...

2 Stir...
   Par...
herbs a...
well, th...
at a tim...

3 Be...
   pea...
mixture...

4 Po...
   sou...
bake i...
minute...

Serves...

Souf...

35 min...

4 large...

30g (1o...

2 tblsp...

¾ cup...

1 cup g...

¼ tspr...

3 eggs...

1 S...
   s...
later...
aside...

MARVELLOUS MEATS

Moist, tender meat dishes can be made with a minimum of fuss as these recipes prove.

Lamb Chops with Mint Pesto

10 minutes

8 wooden skewers, soaked in water for 10 minutes

8 lamb loin chops

2 cloves garlic, chopped

½ cup mint leaves

¼ cup parsley leaves

⅓ cup chopped walnut halves

¼ tspn black pepper

⅓ cup olive oil

1 Skewer each chop to hold neatly in place. Grill the chops on each side until cooked through, about 4 minutes each side.

2 Meanwhile, place the garlic, mint, parsley, walnuts and pepper in a food processor and pulse until just chopped, pouring in oil in a thin stream.

3 Serve chops, with the mint pesto.

Serves 4

Warm Steak Salad with Pawpaw (Papaya) and Spanish Onion

10 minutes

750g (1½lb) fillet steak, trimmed of all fat

1 tblspn finely chopped rosemary

¼ tspn cayenne pepper

2 tblspn unsalted butter

1 small pawpaw (papaya), peeled and cut into bite-size cubes

1 small Spanish onion, thinly sliced

1 small bunch curly endive, torn into bite-size pieces

DRESSING

2 tblspn red wine vinegar

salt

pepper

5 tblspn olive oil

1 To make dressing: Mix vinegar with salt and freshly ground pepper, whisk in oil. Set aside.

2 Cut fillet into thin strips. Sprinkle with rosemary and cayenne pepper. Heat butter in a heavy based frying pan, cook meat over high heat for 1-2 minutes, tossing gently.

3 Mix fillet strips with pawpaw and Spanish onion. Toss well with dressing. Divide endive among 4 plates, mound beef salad in the centre of each lettuce bed. Serve immediately.

Serves 4

Lamb Chops with Mint Pesto

Veal with Coppa

10 minutes

2 tblspn butter

2 tblspn oil

6 veal scallopine

pinch of sage

salt

pepper

6 thin slices coppa (see note)

6 slices mozzarella

1 Heat butter and oil in a heavy based frying pan, cook veal until just done. Remove and place on a ovenproof dish. Sprinkle with sage, season to taste with salt and freshly ground pepper.

2 Cover each scallopine with a slice of coppa, top with mozzarella. Place under a griller until cheese melts. Serve immediately.

Note: Coppa is an Italian cured ham, fattier than prosciutto, and therefore much cheaper. It is made from the shoulder and neck of the pig.

Serves 6

Lamb Fillets with Cassis

15 minutes

2 lamb fillets

1 tblspn butter

6 tblspn Cassis (blackcurrant liqueur)

2 tblspn blackcurrant jelly

1 cup frozen blackcurrants

salt

pepper

1 Trim fillets of all fat and sinews. Brown quickly in melted butter in a heavy based frying pan. Baste with a little Cassis and place in a moderate oven for 8 minutes. Set aside on a warm platter.

2 In the same pan bring to a boil the blackcurrant jelly and remaining Cassis, incorporate pan juices and scraping up any browned bits. Add blackcurrants, season to taste with salt and freshly ground pepper. Cook 1-2 minutes, pour over thinly sliced fillets.

Serves 2

Barbecued Steak Thai-style

6 minutes

3 cloves garlic

1 chilli

1 large onion, quartered

1 bunch coriander, carefully washed

5 tblspn freshly squeezed lime juice

¼ cup nam pla (Oriental fish sauce, available in Oriental food stores and some supermarkets)

2 tblspn brown sugar

salt

6 large minute steaks, or 12 small

1 Blend together garlic, chilli and onion in a processor. Add coriander leaves and a few stems, process until finely chopped. Add lime juice, nam pla and sugar. Season to taste with salt, process a further 30 seconds.

2 Brush both sides of steaks with the mixture and barbecue on high heat for 1-2 minutes, while brushing with mixture constantly.

3 Warm remaining mixture gently and spoon over steaks. Serve immediately.

Serves 6

Pork Strips with Mustard Cream Sauce

25 minutes

2 tblspn butter

1 tblspn oil

750g (1½lb) fillet of pork, cut into strips

1 cup white wine

2 tblspn mustard

1½ cups cream

1 Heat the butter and oil in a large frying pan over moderate heat. Add the pork, cook for 10 minutes, turning frequently.

2 Stir in the wine and mustard and mix thoroughly. Add the cream and increase heat, cook until mixture thickens, about 10 minutes. Serve with rice if desired.

Serves 4

Thyme Pork Medallions with Apples

15 minutes

4 pork medallions, 2cm (¾in) thick

¼ cup flour

4 tblspn butter

2 tblspn finely chopped fresh thyme

2 apples, unpeeled, cut into thin slices

1 Lightly dredge the pork medallions in the flour. Heat the butter in a large frying pan over moderate heat. Cook the medallions for 5 minutes on each side.

2 While the medallions are cooking, sprinkle the thyme over each chop. Remove the medallions and keep warm.

3 Using the same frying pan, saute the apples for 2 minutes, or until just tender, not mushy. Arrange the medallions and apples on serving plate.

Serves 4-6

Pork Strips with Mustard Cream Sauce (top); Thyme Pork Medallions with Apples (bottom)

Beef Salad with Blanched Vegetables

Beef Salad with Blanched Vegetables

40 minutes

2 tblspn butter

350g (11oz) eye fillet of beef

1 cup peeled pumpkin, cut into thin strips

1 cup beans, trimmed

1 cup quartered green baby squash

2 tblspn red capsicum (pepper), cut into small dice

3 tblspn olive oil

1 clove garlic, crushed

3 tblspn red wine vinegar

¼ tspn cracked black pepper

1 Melt butter in a medium frying pan over high heat. Add beef fillet and sear until browned on all sides, about 5 minutes.

2 Transfer fillet to a baking dish and cook in a moderate oven for 30 minutes or until cooked as desired.

3 Meanwhile bring a large saucepan of water to the boil, add the pumpkin, beans and squash, cook for 2 minutes, refresh under cold running water.

4 Cut beef into thin slices and toss with the vegetables, capsicum and combined olive oil, garlic, vinegar and pepper.

Serves 4

Eye Fillet of Beef with Red Capsicum (Pepper) Butter

45 minutes

2 tblspn butter

410g (13oz) eye fillet of beef

125g (4oz) butter, softened, extra

1 tblspn very finely chopped red capsicum (pepper)

2 tblspn freshly grated Parmesan cheese

1 Melt the butter in a medium frying pan over high heat. Add the beef fillet and sear until browned on all sides, about 5 minutes.

2 Transfer fillet to baking dish and cook in a moderate oven for about 35 minutes (for medium).

3 Meanwhile combine extra softened butter with the capsicum and Parmesan cheese, mix well. Spoon mixture onto a sheet of greaseproof paper in a rough log shape, about 2 x 15cm (¾ x 6in). Fold one side of the paper over the roll and gently mould into a neat log; refrigerate until meat is cooked.

4 Slice butter log into ½cm (¼in) thick rounds and serve on the hot sliced beef. Serve immediately.

Serves 4

Eye Fillet of Beef with Red Capsicum (Pepper) Butter

Veal Piccata

20 minutes

¼ cup flour

8 medium veal scallops, tenderised

4 tblspn butter

½ cup freshly squeezed lemon juice

½ cup dry white wine

1 lemon

1 Lightly flour veal on both sides. Shake off excess.

2 Melt the butter in a medium frying pan over moderate heat. When bubbling, add veal and saute about 2 minutes on each side. When the veal is nearly cooked, sprinkle on lemon juice. Remove veal from the frying pan and keep warm.

3 Add wine to the frying pan and boil over high heat, stirring constantly until liquid is reduced to about ¼ cup. Pour sauce over veal.

4 Cut the lemon into paper thin slices and place 3 slices on each veal scallop. Serve immediately.

Serves 4

Eye Fillet with Wild Mushroom Sauce

45 minutes

1 packet dried wild mushrooms

750g (1½lb) eye fillet of beef

2 tblspn Dijon mustard

3 tblspn unsalted butter

2 tblspn finely chopped onion

250g (½lb) button mushrooms, finely sliced

⅓ cup dry Madeira

1 tspn freshly squeezed lemon juice

salt

pepper

1 Preheat oven to 250°C (500°F). Soak wild mushrooms in hot water to cover for 30 minutes.

2 Meanwhile, trim fillet, tie into a neat shape with string. Cover with mustard and small dabs of 1 tablespoon of the butter. Place in the oven for 15 minutes. Turn oven down to 150°C (300°F) and cook a further 15 minutes. Remove and allow to stand.

3 Strain mushrooms. Reserve mushroom soaking water for a future purpose. Saute onion in 1 tablespoon of the butter for 2 minutes, add button mushrooms. Saute over moderate heat for 1 minute.

4 Add Madeira, raise heat. Add lemon juice, season to taste with salt and freshly ground pepper. Swirl in remaining tablespoon butter in small pieces. Pour over fillet, serve immediately.

Serves 4

Veal Cutlets with Balsamic Vinegar and Honey Glaze

10 minutes

6 tblspn balsamic vinegar

3 tspn honey

8 veal cutlets

1 cup dry breadcrumbs

salt

pepper

½ cup olive oil

3 cloves garlic, crushed

2 tblspn unsalted butter

½ cup dry white wine

fresh coriander leaves for garnish

1 Mix together vinegar and honey, stir until honey dissolves. Set aside.

2 Cover cutlets with breadcrumbs and season with salt and freshly ground pepper.

3 In a heavy based frying pan, heat oil until very hot, saute cutlets for 2 minutes on each side. Set aside on a warm platter.

4 Wipe the frying pan with paper towels. Cook garlic in the butter until golden. Add white wine and boil to reduce liquid to 4 tablespoons. Add vinegar and honey mixture and boil until syrupy. Spoon glaze over cutlets and sprinkle with coriander leaves.

Serves 4

Veal with Sun-dried Tomatoes

25 minutes

½ cup marinated sun-dried tomatoes, reserve 4 tblspn of oil

500g (1lb) veal scallops, cut into strips

2 tblspn olive oil

1 red onion, chopped

2 cloves garlic, crushed

1 tomato, finely chopped

200g (6½oz) baby squash, quartered

1 tblspn finely chopped rosemary

2 tblspn tomato paste

½ cup chicken stock

¼ cup dry white wine

1 tspn plain flour

1 tblspn finely chopped parsley

1 Heat the reserved sun-dried tomato oil in a medium frying pan over moderate heat. Add the veal, cook for 1 minute, remove with a slotted spoon and set aside.

2 Add the olive oil to the frying pan, then add the onion, garlic, tomato, squash, rosemary and tomato paste, cook for 2 minutes.

3 Combine the stock, wine and flour and add to the frying pan, cook until reduced by half, about 10 minutes.

4 Stir in the veal, sun-dried tomatoes and parsley, serve immediately.

Serves 4

Veal with Sun-dried Tomatoes (top); Veal Piccata (bottom)

Liver and Coppa Rolls

25 minutes

315g (10 oz) calf's liver

16 thin slices coppa (see note)

3 tblspn freshly squeezed lemon juice

pepper

1 tspn dried thyme

2 tblspn unsalted butter

⅓ cup brandy

8 baby onions

½ cup beef stock

250g (½lb) button mushrooms

1 tblspn finely chopped parsley to garnish

1 Slice the liver into long thin pieces. Place each piece on 2 slices of overlapping coppa, roll up with coppa on the outside. Secure with a toothpick. Sprinkle liver rolls with lemon juice, freshly ground pepper, and thyme.

2 Heat butter in a heavy based frying pan, add rolls and cook until lightly browned. Add brandy and toss gently. Add onions and stock, cook, covered, for 7 minutes. Add mushrooms and cook a further 3 minutes. Serve immediately, sprinkled with parsley.

Note: Coppa is an Italian cured ham, much fattier than prosciutto, but just as delicious. It is made from the shoulder and neck of the pig.

Serves 4

Caramelized Pork Chops

40 minutes — includes marinating time

1 cup brown sugar

1 cup cider vinegar

8 tblspn vegetable oil

8 pork chops

½ cup dry sherry

8 tblspn walnut oil

1 cup walnut halves

1 cup dried apricots

1 Combine sugar and vinegar, stir until sugar is dissolved. Marinate chops 15-20 minutes in this mixture.

2 Heat oil in a heavy based frying pan. Add chops and saute over high heat, 4 minutes each side. Remove to a warm plate. Deglaze pan with sherry. Reduce liquid to 2 tablespoons.

3 In another pan heat walnut oil and saute walnuts until golden brown. Add oil and nuts to deglazed pan, together with dried apricots. Cook gently for 1-2 minutes. Return chops and simmer in the sauce 3-4 minutes or until heated through. Spoon sauce over chops and serve immediately.

Serves 4

Rack of Lamb with Mustard Herb Crust

40 minutes

2 racks of baby lamb, 6 chops each

1 cup fresh white breadcrumbs

½ cup finely chopped parsley

¼ cup finely chopped rosemary

1 clove garlic, crushed

2 tblspn Dijon mustard

2 tblspn olive oil

1 Trim rack of lamb, leaving the rib bones as long as possible. Leave about 0.5cm (¼in) of fat on the outside of the rack.

2 In a small bowl, combine breadcrumbs, parsley, rosemary, garlic, mustard and olive oil. Set aside.

3 Place the racks of lamb in a baking dish and cook for 15 minutes in a moderate oven. Remove and press the breadcrumbs mixture on top of the rack and on the bony side to form a crust.

4 Return to the oven for another 10 to 15 minutes.

Serves 4

Rack of Lamb with Mustard Herb Crust

YOUR 'QUICK SMART' STORE CUPBOARD

When you're short of time in the kitchen, it's a help to have all the basic ingredients to hand. Why not stock up with these staples so that you'll always have what's required when you need it. If you buy a little often, you'll hardly notice any extra costs.

Biscuits and Grains

Biscuits for cheese
Corn chips for dips
Breadcrumbs
Plain flour
Self-raising flour
Wholemeal flour
Pasta and noodles —
spaghetti, fettucine,
macaroni, fussili, spinach
pasta, egg noodles
Plain long-grain rice
Basmati rice
Arborio rice
Bulgur
Tortillas
Poppadoms

Sauces and Condiments

Tomato ketchup
Tobasco sauce
Chilli sauce
Sambal oelek (chilli paste)
Angostura bitters
Mayonnaise
Dijon mustard
Wholegrain mustard
Dry mustard
Horseradish
Olive oil
Walnut oil
Vegetable oil
Vinaigrette
Pesto
Soy sauce
Tamari
Peeled Italian tomatoes
Tomato paste
Chicken, beef and
vegetable stock cubes
Vinegar, white, red wine,
white wine, tarragon and
cider
Worcestershire sauce
Sun-dried tomatoes
Salt, cooking salt, sea salt
Peppercorns
Cracked black pepper
Herbs and spices
Curry Powder
Chutney
Gherkins

Frozen Foods

Home-made stocks
Fresh breadcrumbs
Peas
Broad beans
Butter
Margarine
Bacon
Pancetta
Filo pastry
Puff pastry
Bread rolls
Orange juice concentrate

Canned Foods

Anchovies
Crabmeat
Salmon
Prawns (shrimp)
Tuna
Artichoke hearts
Pimentos
Bamboo shoots
Hearts of palm
Beans
Olives
Water chestnuts
Consomme
Fruits

For Baking

Sugar, granulated, brown,
castor, icing sugar
Corn syrup
Maple syrup
Jam, jelly, preserves
Desiccated coconut
Unsweetened cocoa
powder
Instant coffee powder
Choc Bits
Raisins
Nuts — almonds, pecans,
peanuts, walnuts
Oil — vegetable, peanut
Vegetable shortening —
copha
Gelatine
Bi-carbonate of soda
Baking soda
Baking powder

Wines and Spirits

Brandy
Coffee Liqueur
Dry red wine
Dry white wine
Orange liqueur (Grand
Marnier, Cointreau)
Rum
Dry sherry
Vermouth
Vodka

Cheeses

Cheddar
Parmesan
Gruyere
Blue-vein cheese
Camembert
Brie
Cream cheese

ENTERTAINING MENUS

With our busy life-styles, it is not always possible to spend hours in the kitchen preparing dinner party dishes. Here are eight menus, especially designed for the busy cook, that are quick to prepare and thoroughly delicious.

MENU 1

Cream of Parsnip Sauce

Chicken and Artichoke Saute with Prosciutto

Creamy Garlic Mashed Potato

Fresh Fruit with Yoghurt and Honey

MENU 2

Avocado with Seafood

Radicchio and Endive Salad with Red Wine Vinaigrette

Veal Scallopini with Sage

Spicy Baked Pears

MENU 3

Hummus Dip

Vegetable Saute with Goat's Cheese

Herbed Lamb Patties

Julienne Melon with Lemon Mint Dressing

MENU 4

Chunky Vegetable Tomato Soup

Salmon Poached in White Wine with Lemon Dill Butter

Grated Zucchini (Courgette) Saute

Apricot Meringue

MENU 5

Smoked Trout and Caviar Dip

Beef Slices with Garlic Worcestershire Sauce

Peas with Prosciutto and Pinenuts

Peach Clafouti

MENU 6

Melon with Prosciutto and Lemon Vinaigrette

Linguine with Prawns (Shrimp) and Olives

Radicchio with Peas

Lemon Souffle Omelette

MENU 7

Chilled Creamy Avocado Soup

Chicken and Snowpea Salad with Water Chestnuts

Potato Slices with Dill

Apple and Blackberry Crumble

MENU 8

Prosciutto Pizzas

Bream Fillets with Sweet Capsicum (Pepper)

Herbed Potatoes

Pears with Blueberry Raspberry Coulis

Cream of Parsnip Soup

*Chicken and Artichoke
Saute with Prosciutto*

*Creamy Garlic Mashed
Potato*

*Fresh Fruit with Yoghurt
and Honey*

Cream of Parsnip Soup

35 minutes

2 tblspn butter

2 onions, peeled and chopped

1½ cups peeled and chopped parsnip

1 medium potato, peeled and chopped

4 cups chicken stock

1 tspn ground pepper

2 tblspn chopped fresh parsley

1 Melt butter in a large saucepan over moderate heat. Add the onion, parsnip and potato, cook gently for 5 minutes.

2 Add the stock and pepper, bring to the boil, reduce heat and simmer for 20 minutes or until vegetables are tender.

3 Puree the soup in a blender or food processor, return soup to saucepan and heat through. Stir in parsley and serve.

Serves 4

Cream of Parsnip Soup

Chicken and Artichoke Saute with Prosciutto

15 minutes

3 tblspn olive oil

4 double chicken fillets, cut into 2cm (¾in) cubes

1 onion, roughly chopped

1 clove garlic, crushed

200g (6½oz) prosciutto, finely chopped

1 cup halved artichoke hearts

½ cup stuffed olives, halved

3 tblspn dry white wine

1 tblspn chopped thyme

1 tblspn chopped basil

1 Heat the oil in a large frying pan over moderate heat, add the chicken, onion and garlic and cook, stirring constantly, for 2 minutes.

2 Add the prosciutto, artichoke hearts, olives, wine, thyme and basil, cook for a further 3 minutes. Serve immediately.

Serves 4

Chicken and Artichoke Saute with Prosciutto (top); Creamy Garlic Mashed Potato (bottom)

Fresh Fruit with Yoghurt and Honey

Creamy Garlic Mashed Potato

25 minutes

5 large potatoes, peeled and chopped

2 tblspn butter

1 clove garlic, crushed

2 tblspn butter, extra

¼ cup cream

½ tspn ground nutmeg

a pinch of paprika

1 tblspn chopped parsley

1 Bring a large saucepan of water to the boil, add the potatoes, cook until tender, about 15 minutes. Drain.

2 Melt the butter in a medium frying pan over moderate heat, add the garlic and cook for 1 minute. Add extra butter, cream and nutmeg to the potatoes and mash until smooth.

3 Spoon potato into serving dish, sprinkle with paprika and parsley.

Serves 4

Fresh Fruit with Yoghurt and Honey

10 minutes

2 bananas, peeled and sliced

1 tblspn freshly squeezed lemon juice

3 oranges, segmented

½ cup raspberries

1 cup natural yoghurt

1 tblspn honey

1 Place bananas in a medium bowl, sprinkle with the lemon juice and toss.

2 Arrange the banana slices, orange segments and raspberries in serving dishes. Top with a serving of yoghurt and drizzle with honey.

Serves 4

Menu 2

Avocado with Seafood

Radicchio and Endive Salad with Red Wine Vinaigrette

Veal Scallopini with Sage

Spicy Baked Pears

Avocado with Seafood

10 minutes

2 ripe avocados

1 tblspn freshly squeezed lemon juice

¼ cup sour cream

3 tblspn mayonnaise

¼ tspn cayenne pepper

155g (5oz) school prawns (shrimp), cooked and peeled

1 tblspn finely chopped continental parsley

8 lemon slices

1 Cut the avocados in half and remove the stones. Scoop out the flesh carefully, reserving skins, and blend or process with the lemon juice, sour cream, mayonnaise and cayenne pepper.

2 Puree until smooth, stir in the peeled prawns and spoon mixture into the avocado skins. Garnish with the chopped parsley and lemon slices.

Serves 4

Avocado with Seafood

Radicchio and Endive Salad with Red Wine Vinaigrette

5 minutes

1 radicchio lettuce, washed and torn into pieces

1 small curly endive, washed and torn into pieces

10 baby yellow squash, cut into thin strips

3 tblspn red wine

2 tblspn red wine vinegar

3 tblspn olive oil

2 cloves garlic, crushed

¼ tspn ground black pepper

1 Arrange the radicchio and endive leaves in a salad bowl.

2 Sprinkle the squash strips over the top and pour over combined red wine, red wine vinegar, olive oil, garlic and pepper.

Serves 4

Veal Scallopini with Sage

10 minutes

8 medium veal scallops

¼ cup plain flour

3 tblspn butter

2 cloves garlic, crushed

3 tblspn wine

2 tblspn chopped fresh sage

1 Lightly dust the veal scallops with the flour.

2 Melt the butter in a large frying pan over moderate heat. Add the garlic and cook for 1 minute. Add the wine and cook for a further 1 minute.

3 Add the sage and veal scallops, cook for 2 minutes each side or until just cooked. Serve immediately with blanched vegetables if desired.

Serves 4

Radicchio and Endive Salad with Red Wine Vinaigrette (top); Veal Scallopini with Sage (bottom)

Spicy Baked Pears

Spicy Baked Pears

30 minutes

6 medium ripe pears

¼ cup butter, melted

1 tspn ground cinnamon

¼ tspn ground cloves

¼ tspn ground nutmeg

4 tblspn brown sugar

mint to garnish

1 Peel the pears, remove and discard cores, slice the flesh into 1cm (½in) slices. Place pear slices in a greased baking dish.

2 Pour over combined melted butter, cinnamon, cloves and nutmeg, sprinkle the sugar over the top.

3 Bake in a moderate oven for 25 minutes or until pears are tender. Serve warm and garnish with mint sprigs if desired.

Serves 6

MENU 3

Hummus Dip

Vegetable Saute with Goat's Cheese

Herbed Lamb Patties

Julienne Melon with Lemon Mint Dressing

Hummus Dip

5 minutes

2 cups drained canned chickpeas

2 cloves garlic, crushed

¼ cup freshly squeezed lemon juice

2 tblspn olive oil

½ cup tahini (see note)

¼ tspn paprika

1 tblspn chopped parsley

2 tblspn olive oil, extra

4 small rounds of pita bread

1 In a blender or food processor, combine the chickpeas, garlic, lemon juice, olive oil and tahini until smooth.

2 Spread hummus on a flat serving plate, sprinkle paprika and parsley on top and drizzle extra olive oil over the top. Serve with pita bread.

Note: Tahini is a sesame paste, available in health food stores.

Serves 4

Hummus Dip

Vegetable Saute with Goat's Cheese

10-15 minutes

¼ cup olive oil

2 cloves garlic, crushed

3 medium carrots, peeled, cut into thin strips

1 red onion, peeled and chopped

1 eggplant (aubergine), cut into 2cm (¾in) cubes

1 red capsicum (pepper), seeds removed, cut into strips

2 tblspn dry red wine

1 tblspn balsamic vinegar

155g (5oz) goat's cheese, crumbled

1 Heat the oil in a large frying pan over moderate heat. Add the garlic and carrots, cook for 2 minutes, stirring constantly.

2 Add the onion, eggplant and capsicum, cook for a further 3 minutes. Add the wine and vinegar, cook for a further 1 minute.

3 Spoon sauteed vegetables into a serving dish and sprinkle with goat's cheese.

Serves 4

Herbed Lamb Patties

15 minutes

2 tblspn butter

2 cloves garlic, crushed

¼ cup finely chopped spring onions (scallions)

750g (1½lb) minced lamb

1 tblspn finely chopped fresh thyme

1 tblspn finely chopped fresh rosemary

1 tblspn finely chopped fresh parsley

1 tblspn freshly squeezed lemon juice

1 tblspn tomato paste

3 tblspn breadcrumbs

Vegetable Saute with Goat's Cheese (top); Herbed Lamb Patties (bottom)

Julienne Melon with Lemon Mint Dressing

1 Heat the butter in a medium frying pan over moderate heat. Add the garlic and spring onions, cook for 1 minute.

2 In a medium bowl, combine the spring onions and garlic with the lamb, thyme, rosemary, parsley, lemon juice, tomato paste and breadcrumbs, mix well.

3 Shape mixture into 12 patties and grill for 3-4 minutes on each side or until cooked through, under medium heat.

Serves 4

Julienne Melon with Lemon Mint Dressing

10 minutes

1 small honeydew melon

¾ cup large strawberries, hulled, cut into small strips

2 tblspn chopped fresh mint

2 tblspn freshly squeezed lemon juice

3 tblspn freshly squeezed orange juice

1 tblspn honey

1 tblspn sesame seeds

1 Peel the honeydew melon and remove seeds. Cut the flesh into 2-3cm (¾-1¼ in) thin strips. Arrange the melon strips and strawberry strips in 4 serving glasses.

2 In a small bowl, combine the mint, lemon juice, orange juice, honey and sesame seeds, mix well. Pour lemon mint dressing over fruit and serve.

Serves 4

MENU 4

Chunky Vegetable Tomato Soup

Salmon Poached in White Wine with Lemon Dill Butter

Grated Zucchini (Courgette) Saute

Apricot Meringue

Chunky Vegetable Tomato Soup

30 minutes

3 tblspn butter

2 onions, peeled and chopped

2 large carrots, peeled, cut into thick strips

2 celery stalks, sliced

¼ cup white wine

2 x 425g (13½oz) cans tinned peeled tomatoes and juice

1 tspn sugar

2 cups chicken stock

2 tblspn chopped fresh basil

1 Melt the butter in a large saucepan over moderate heat. Add the onions, carrots and celery, cook stirring constantly for 2 minutes.

2 Add the wine and cook for a further 1 minute. Stir in the tinned tomatoes and chop tomatoes with the edge of wooden spoon.

3 Add the sugar and stock, simmer for 15 minutes. Serve soup with fresh chopped basil.

Serves 4

Chunky Vegetable Tomato Soup

Salmon Poached in White Wine with Lemon Dill Butter

25 minutes

125g (4oz) butter, softened

1 tblspn chopped fresh dill

2 tblspn freshly squeezed lemon juice

1 clove garlic, crushed

1 cup chicken stock

1 cup dry white wine

1 tspn ground black pepper

4 salmon cutlets

1 To make the lemon dill butter: Mix the softened butter with the dill, lemon juice and garlic, mix well until combined and butter is light. Set aside at room temperature.

2 Heat the chicken stock, wine and pepper in a large frying pan over moderate heat. When simmering, add the salmon cutlets and simmer for 4 minutes each side, or until cooked through.

3 Drain cutlets and serve immediately with the lemon butter.

Serves 4

Grated Zucchini (Courgette) Saute

7 minutes

3 tblspn butter

1 small onion, peeled and grated

¼ tspn ground nutmeg

3 large zucchini (courgette), grated

1 Melt the butter in a medium frying pan over moderate heat, add the onion and cook for 1-2 minutes, do not brown.

2 Stir in the nutmeg, then toss the zucchini in the hot onion butter until tender. Serve immediately.

Serves 4

Grated Zucchini (Courgette) Saute (top); Salmon Poached in White Wine with Lemon Dill Butter (bottom)

Apricot Meringue

Apricot Meringue

45 minutes

3 cups tinned apricot halves, drained

2 tblspn brandy

2 tspn vanilla essence

3 tblspn castor sugar

3 eggs, separated

¼ cup castor sugar, extra

1 Blend or process apricot halves with the brandy, vanilla, sugar and egg yolks until smooth, about 1 minute. Pour mixture into a greased 20cm (8in) round ovenproof dish.

2 Bake in a moderate oven for 8 minutes, remove from heat and set aside.

3 Beat the egg-whites and extra sugar with an electric mixer until soft peaks form. Carefully spread meringue over the pre-cooked apricot base. Return to moderate oven and cook for a further 20 minutes.

Serves 4

MENU 5

Smoked Trout and Caviar Dip

Beef Slices with Garlic Worcestershire Sauce

Peas with Prosciutto and Pinenuts

Peach Clafouti

Smoked Trout and Caviar Dip

10 minutes

300g (10oz) whole smoked trout

3 tblspn freshly squeezed lemon juice

½ tspn ground black pepper

3 tblspn sour cream

250g (½lb) cottage cheese

4 tblspn red caviar

4 tblspn black caviar

watercress sprig, to garnish

1 Carefully peel skin away from trout, cut off head and remove bones. Mash the trout flesh in a medium bowl with the lemon juice, pepper and sour cream. Stir cottage cheese into trout mixture and combine.

2 Spoon mixture into serving dish and smooth with a knife. Spoon the red caviar onto one side of the smoothed dip and the black caviar onto the other side. Using a knife, carefully spread the caviar evenly over the top.

3 Garnish with a sprig of watercress and serve with rusks or French bread.

Serves 4

Smoked Trout and Caviar Dip

Beef Slices with Garlic Worcestershire Sauce

10 minutes

1kg (2lb) beef eye fillet, trimmed

3 tblspn butter

2 cloves garlic, crushed

3 tspn brown sugar

2 tblspn red wine vinegar

4 tblspn Worcestershire sauce

sesame seeds, to garnish

1 Slice the eye fillet of beef into 2cm (¾in) thick medallions. Place each medallion between 2 pieces of plastic wrap and pound with a mallet until medallions are ½cm (¼in) thick.

2 Heat the butter in a large frying pan over moderate heat. Add the garlic, sugar, vinegar and Worcestershire sauce, cook for 1 minute.

3 Add the beef scallops to the frying pan and cook until just tender, about 1 minute each side. Remove beef with a slotted spoon and keep warm.

4 Bring pan juices to a boil, reduce heat and simmer until sauce thickens, about 1-2 minutes.

5 Pour sauce over beef and sprinkle with sesame seeds. Serve immediately with a side salad if desired.

Serves 4

Peas with Prosciutto and Pinenuts (top); Beef Slices with Garlic Worcestershire Sauce (bottom)

Peach Clafouti

Peas with Prosciutto and Pinenuts

10-12 minutes

2 tblspn butter

1 tspn sugar

1½ cups frozen peas, thawed

2 tblspn olive oil

1 clove garlic, crushed

½ cup prosciutto, cut into short strips

3 tblspn pinenuts

1 Place the butter and sugar in a medium saucepan of boiling water. Add the peas and cook until just tender, about 3 minutes; drain the peas.

2 Heat the oil in a medium frying pan over moderate heat. Add the garlic, prosciutto and pinenuts, cook, stirring constantly, until pinenuts are golden.

3 Stir drained peas into prosciutto mixture, toss well; serve immediately.

Serves 4

Peach Clafouti

55 minutes

1 tblspn butter

2 tblspn sugar

¾ cup milk

¼ cup thickened cream

3 eggs

½ cup sugar, extra

1 tspn vanilla essence

pinch of salt

⅔ cup plain flour

2 x 425g (13½oz) cans peach slices, drained

1 Grease a 20cm (8in) ovenproof flan dish with butter and dust the bottom with the sugar.

2 In a blender or food processor, combine the milk, cream, eggs, extra sugar, vanilla, salt and flour. Blend at high speed for 1 minute.

3 Pour ½ cup batter into the dish. Arrange the peach slices over it in an even layer and pour the remaining batter over the peaches.

4 Bake in a moderate oven for 45 minutes or until the top is golden brown and the batter is set. Serve immediately.

Serves 4-6

MENU 6

Melon with Prosciutto and
Lemon Vinaigrette

Linguine with Prawns
(Shrimp) and Olives

Radicchio with Peas

Lemon Souffle Omelette

Melon with Prosciutto and Lemon Vinaigrette

20 minutes

½ medium rockmelon

20 very thin slices of prosciutto

VINAIGRETTE

3 tblspn freshly squeezed lemon juice

5 tblspn olive oil

1 tblspn fresh chives, chopped

1 tspn cracked black pepper

1 Peel rockmelon, remove seeds and cut into 1cm (½in) thick wedges. Cut each wedge in half crossways and wrap with a slice of prosciutto. Continue with all melon pieces and prosciutto, then arrange decoratively on serving plate.

2 To make vinaigrette: Mix together the lemon juice, olive oil, chives and pepper, pour over melon.

Serves 4

Melon with Prosciutto and Lemon Vinaigrette

Linguine with Prawns (Shrimp) and Olives

20 minutes

315g (10oz) linguine

4 tblspn butter

2 cloves garlic, crushed

1 large onion, peeled and chopped

3 tblspn pitted and chopped black olives

3 cups tinned tomatoes and their juice

1 tspn sugar

1 tblspn tomato paste

2 tspn dried rosemary, chopped

315g (10oz) medium uncooked prawns (shrimp), peeled, tails intact, deveined

¼ cup freshly grated Parmesan cheese

2 tblspn finely chopped fresh parsley

1 Bring a large saucepan of water to the boil, add the linguine and cook until just tender, drain, set aside.

2 Melt the butter in a large frying pan over moderate heat. Add the garlic, onion and olives, cook for 3 minutes, stirring constantly.

3 Add the tomatoes and their juice, sugar, tomato paste and rosemary, cook for a further 5 minutes.

4 Add the prawns and cook for a further 3 minutes.

5 Add the linguine to the sauce and toss well. Serve with Parmesan cheese and parsley.

Serves 4

Radicchio with Peas

10 minutes

2 cups frozen peas, thawed

2 tblspn butter

2 tblspn honey

1 tblspn freshly squeezed lemon juice

8 radicchio leaves, shredded

1 Bring a large saucepan of water to the boil, add the peas and cook for 2 minutes, drain and refresh under cold water, drain again.

Radicchio with Peas (top); Linguine with Prawns (Shrimp) and Olives (bottom)

Lemon Souffle Omelette

2 Melt the butter in a small saucepan, over a moderate heat. Add the honey and lemon juice, cook for 1 minute or until combined. Toss the peas and lettuce in the honey butter, serve immediately.

Serves 4

Lemon Souffle Omelette

10 minutes

2 eggs, separated

2 tblspn cream

4 tblspn castor sugar

1 tblspn freshly squeezed lemon juice

1 tblspn freshly squeezed lime juice

1 tblspn butter

icing sugar, for dusting

1 Using an electric mixer, beat the egg yolks, cream, sugar, lemon juice and lime juice for 1 minute.

2 In a separate bowl, beat the egg-whites until soft peaks form. Fold the egg yolk mixture into the whites, one tablespoon at a time.

3 Melt the butter in a medium frying pan until sizzling. Pour the omelette into the frying pan, cook until golden underneath, about 2 minutes.

4 Transfer frying pan to grill and cook until top of omelette is dry to touch. Using a spatula, ease omelette onto serving plate, fold in half and dust with icing sugar. Serve with fresh cream and blueberries if desired.

Makes 1

MENU 7

*Chilled Creamy Avocado
Soup*

*Chicken and Snowpea
Salad with Water Chestnuts*

Potato Slices with Dill

*Apple and Blackberry
Crumble*

Chilled Creamy
Avocado Soup

10 minutes

3 medium very ripe avocados, peeled and
seeded

4 tblspn chopped spring onions (scallions)

1 green chilli, chopped

3 tblspn freshly squeezed lemon juice

3 cups cold milk

1 Place avocado flesh, spring
onions, chilli and lemon juice in
a blender or food processor, blend
until smooth. While motor is running
slowly add the milk.

2 Season to taste and refrigerate
until ready to serve.

Serves 4

Chilled Creamy Avocado Soup

Chicken and Snowpea Salad with Water Chestnuts

15 minutes

200g (6½oz) snowpeas, trimmed

1 barbecued chicken, skin and bones removed

1 red capsicum (pepper), seeded, cut into thin strips

200g (6½oz) tin sliced water chestnuts, drained

3 tblspn freshly squeezed orange juice

2 tblspn freshly squeezed lemon juice

½ tspn chilli paste (sambal oelek)

1 tblspn chopped chives

4 tblspn olive oil

1 Bring a medium saucepan of water to the boil, add snowpeas, cook for 30 seconds, remove with a slotted spoon, refresh under cold water, drain.

2 Break chicken into bite-size pieces and arrange on serving plate with blanched snowpeas, capsicum strips and water chestnuts.

3 Mix the orange juice, lemon juice, chilli paste, chives and olive oil together until well combined and pour over salad.

Serves 4

Potato Slices with Dill (above left); Chicken and Snowpea Salad with Water Chestnuts (above right)

Potato Slices with Dill

15 minutes

12 baby potatoes

2 tblspn butter, melted

2 tblspn chopped fresh dill

1 Peel potatoes and cut into 0.5cm (¼in) slices. Bring a large saucepan of water to the boil, add potato slices and cook for 7 minutes or until just tender. Drain and refresh quickly under cold water.

2 Arrange potato slices on a serving plate, drizzle melted butter over them and sprinkle with the dill.

Serves 4

Apple and Blackberry Crumble

Apple and Blackberry Crumble

30 minutes

2½ cups tinned pie apple

1½ cups fresh blackberries

1 tblspn brown sugar

1 cup plain flour

½ cup castor sugar

125g (1oz) butter, cut into tiny cubes

1 In a medium bowl, gently combine the apples, blackberries and brown sugar. Divide the mixture between four 1-cup capacity ovenproof dishes.

2 Mix together the flour, castor sugar and butter, using the tips of the fingers until mixture resembles fine breadcrumbs.

3 Sprinkle over the fruit in each dish and bake in a moderate oven for 20 minutes. Serve with cream if desired.

Serves 4

Prosciutto Pizzas

Prosciutto Pizzas

15 minutes

2 rosetta rolls, cut in half

3 tblspn tomato paste

8 slices prosciutto

4 slices mozzarella cheese, each ¼cm (1/8in) thick

2 tblspn red capsicum (pepper), seeded and finely chopped

2 tblspn chopped parsley

1 Spread each half roll with the tomato paste, top with the prosciutto, then cheese, red capsicum and parsley.

2 Bake in a moderate oven for 10 minutes or until cheese has melted.

Serves 4

Bream Fillets with Sweet Capsicum (Pepper)

15 minutes

4 bream fillets, 200g (6½oz) each

½ cup flour

4 tblspn unsalted butter

2 cloves garlic, crushed

1 red capsicum (pepper), seeded, cut into thin strips

1 green capsicum (pepper), seeded, cut into thin strips

3 chillis, seeded, cut into thin strips

1 onion, sliced

3 tblspn white wine vinegar

¼ cup chicken stock

1 Dip each fillet in the flour. Melt the butter in a large frying pan over moderate heat, add the fillets, cook for 2 minutes each side, remove and keep warm in a low oven.

2 Add the garlic, capsicum, chillis, onion, vinegar and stock to the frying pan. Bring to the boil and simmer for 5 minutes.

3 Serve capsicum sauce over fish.

Serves 4

Herbed Potatoes

30 minutes

12 baby potatoes, cut in halves

¼ cup butter, melted

3 tblspn oil

2 tspn salt

1 tblspn dried mixed herbs

1 Bring a large saucepan of water to the boil, add the potatoes and cook for 7 minutes. Drain and toss in the combined butter, oil, salt and herbs.

2 Place potatoes in a baking dish and cook in a moderately hot oven for 10-15 minutes or until golden.

Serves 4

Bream Fillet with Sweet Capsicum (Pepper) (top); Herbed Potatoes (bottom)

Pears with Blueberry Raspberry Coulis

Pears with Blueberry Raspberry Coulis

10-15 minutes

½ cup blueberries

1 cup raspberries

4 tblspn freshly squeezed orange juice

2 tblspn icing sugar

12 canned pear halves, drained

¾ cup blueberries, extra

¼ cup thickened cream

1 To make coulis: Place blueberries, raspberries, orange juice and icing sugar in a blender or food processor, blend until smooth. Push mixture through a sieve and discard the pips. Spoon the coulis onto each serving plate.

2 Arrange the pear halves and extra blueberries on the coulis.

3 Place four small droplets of cream on the coulis. Carefully pull a skewer through the coulis and through the centre of each droplet without lifting the skewer out of the sauce.

Serves 4

QUICK SMART TIPS GREAT TIME-SAVING IDEAS

- For a quick salad: Always keep several cans of fruit in the refrigerator. When needed, drain and serve tossed with some salad greens, herbs and dressing.
- *Mise en place*: This French expression means "to set out every ingredient we need for the recipe neatly, measured and ready for the cook to use". Once you get used to doing this, it makes cooking a breeze.
- When buying chicken for a recipe which calls for boned chicken, buy breast fillets or thigh fillets. Although more expensive, these are already boned and trimmed and will save you valuable time.
- When buying canned salmon, always go for the skinless, boneless variety.
- Line your grill tray with foil. After grilling greasy chops or sausages, discard and replace with a new piece. The griller tray stays clean.
- For quicker measuring of butter, just remember one packet is 250 grams, which is half a pound. When a recipe calls for 125g (4oz) butter, this means half the packet. When a recipe calls for 4 tablespoons, this means one third of the packet; 3 tablespoons means one quarter of the packet.

- Always turn on the oven before you begin preparations. This way it will be pre-heated by the time you need it.
- When making a pasta dish, always start to boil the water first. This takes a long time, so do it while preparing the sauce.
- If in a really great hurry, use hot water from the tap.
- Use pots and pans for cooking which are attractive enough to go straight to the table.
- Get into the habit of cooking double quantities of dishes which freeze well, such as soups, curries and stews.

- Have a good supply of stocks in your freezer.
- Never throw out odds and ends of bread. Make crumbs and keep in a sealed container in the freezer. Fresh breadcrumbs can transform an otherwise ordinary dish.
- Make large quantities of your favourite salad dressing. Keep in the refrigerator in an airtight jar, shake well before using.
- One of the greatest time-savers in the kitchen is a microwave oven. Used together with your freezer, it will enable you to cook when you have the time and defrost in a hurry.

- On the subject of equipment, remember that having the right tool for the job always saves time.
- A set of good knives — bread knife, paring knife, chopping knife and carving knife — is an indispensable help to the cook.
- The same goes for pots and pans. You need a large pan for cooking pasta, a small one for boiling eggs. And try to buy the best quality utensils you can afford, you'll save in the long run.

PLEASING POULTRY

Poultry dishes are among the quickest to make as the meat takes little time to cook. The subtle flavours in these quick poultry recipes are sure to please.

Chicken Breasts with Lemon and Brandy

12 minutes

½ cup plain flour

1 tblspn finely chopped chives

salt

pepper

6 boneless chicken breast halves

155g (5oz) unsalted butter

⅓ cup freshly squeezed lemon juice

⅓ cup brandy

3 tblspn chopped parsley

1 Combine flour, chives, salt and freshly ground pepper in a deep plate. Dredge chicken in the seasoned flour, shake off excess.

2 Melt half the butter in a heavy based pan. When foaming, add chicken and saute 4 minutes on each side. Add lemon juice and brandy. Ignite and when flame subsides, remove chicken to a warm platter.

3 Whisk remaining butter into sauce, 1 tablespoon at a time, pour over chicken. Sprinkle with parsley and serve immediately.

Serves 6

Peppered Chicken Breast Fillets

25 minutes

2 tblspn cracked black pepper

4 double chicken fillets

4 tblspn butter

½ cup Madeira

1 cup cream

1 Sprinkle the pepper on each side of the chicken fillets and lightly pound pepper into the chicken.

2 Melt the butter in a large frying pan over moderate heat. Add the chicken breasts, cook for 1 minute each side, or until chicken is only just cooked. Transfer chicken to an ovenproof dish and keep warm in a low oven.

3 Meanwhile, add the Madeira and cream to the frying pan. Bring sauce to the boil and simmer until reduced by half. Pour sauce over chicken.

Serves 4

Peppered Chicken Breast Fillets

Chicken Livers with Ginger

8 minutes

¼ cup soy sauce

2 tblspn brandy

1 tspn brown sugar

1 tspn grated fresh ginger

1 clove garlic, finely chopped

3 tblspn butter

1 onion, thinly sliced

500g (1lb) chicken livers

flour

salt

pepper

2 tblspn chopped parsley

1 Combine soy sauce, brandy, brown sugar, ginger and garlic in a bowl.

2 Melt half the butter in a heavy based pan, add onions and cook until translucent.

3 Dredge livers in flour, sprinkle with salt and freshly ground pepper. Add remaining butter to the pan, when foaming add livers and brown for 1 minute.

4 Add soy sauce mixture, cook, basting frequently, until livers are cooked, about 2 minutes. Sprinkle with parsley, serve immediately.

Serves 4

Orange Chicken

15 minutes

1 large orange

4 boneless, skinless chicken breast halves

2 tblspn unsalted butter

2 tblspn chopped onion

⅓ cup port

½ cup orange marmalade

½ cup heavy cream

2 tblspn Dijon mustard

2 tblspn chopped fresh chives

1 Peel orange, cut into dice and place in a bowl.

Chicken Stroganoff

2 Pound chicken breasts between waxed paper until flattened to 0.5cm (¼ in) thick.

3 Melt butter in a heavy based pan. When it foams, add chicken breasts and saute 3 minutes on each side. Transfer to a warm dish and cover.

4 Pour off all but 1 tablespoon of fat. Add onion and cook 1 minute. Add port, orange dice and any juice in bowl, and marmalade. Bring to a boil, scraping up any browned bits.

5 Add cream and mustard, cook, stirring occasionally, until sauce thickens, about 3 minutes.

6 Pour sauce over chicken and sprinkle with chives.

Serves 4

Baked Herbed Chicken

36 minutes

6 chicken fillets

6 tblspn chopped coriander

12 tblspn freshly squeezed lime juice

2 cloves garlic, finely chopped

pepper

6 tblspn unsalted butter

6 tblspn chopped parsley

1 Pre-heat oven to 190°C (375°F).

2 Place each fillet on a large piece of foil. Sprinkle with 1 tablespoon of coriander each, add 2 tablespoons lime juice, sprinkle of garlic and freshly ground pepper. Top with 1 tablespoon butter and 1 tablespoon parsley.

3 Fold foil into neat parcels, seal securely. Bake in pre-heated oven for 30 minutes. Serve in foil.

Serves 6

Honey Soy Sauce Chicken Wings (top); Redcurrant Glazed Spatchcock (bottom)

Honey Soy Sauce Chicken Wings

15 minutes

3 tblspn butter

1 clove garlic, crushed

1 tblspn grated fresh ginger

16 chicken wings

3 tblspn honey

¼ cup Worcestershire sauce

3 tblspn soy sauce

3 tblspn sesame seeds

1 Melt the butter in a large frying pan over moderate heat. Add the garlic and ginger, cook for 1 minute.

2 Add the chicken wings to the pan and toss them in the butter, garlic and ginger, cook for 3 minutes.

3 Add the honey, Worcestershire sauce and soy sauce and cook until sauce thickens and chicken wings are cooked, about 5 minutes.

4 Add sesame seeds to the pan and mix well.

Serves 4

Chicken Stroganoff

30 minutes

50g (1¾oz) butter

500g (1lb) chicken fillet, cut into strips

30g (1oz) butter, extra

155g (5oz) button mushrooms, halved

½ cup dry white wine

1 cup thickened cream

2 tblspn tomato paste

½ tspn ground nutmeg

1 tblspn finely chopped spring onions (scallions)

1 Melt the butter in a large frying pan over moderate heat. Add the chicken strips and cook, stirring constantly, for 2 minutes or until cooked on the outside only. Remove chicken from frying pan with a slotted spoon and set aside.

2 Add the extra butter to the frying pan, cook mushrooms for 1 minute. Add the wine, cream, tomato paste and nutmeg and cook for 5 minutes over high heat or until sauce thickens slightly.

3 Add the chicken to the frying pan, toss in sauce and cook for a further 1 minute. Stir in spring onions and serve immediately.

Serves 4

Redcurrant Glazed Spatchcock

35 minutes

4 spatchcocks, cut in half lengthwise

REDCURRANT GLAZE

1 tblspn butter

4 tblspn redcurrant jelly

2 tspn honey

3 tblspn freshly squeezed lemon juice

1 To make redcurrant glaze: Heat the butter, redcurrant jelly, honey and lemon juice in a small saucepan over moderate heat. Stir until ingredients are well combined.

2 Brush both sides of each spatchcock half with the redcurrant glaze. Bake in a moderate oven for 25 minutes, basting regularly with remaining glaze.

Serves 4

Crusty Parmesan Chicken Drumsticks (above); Sauteed Chicken Breasts in Curry Cream Sauce (right)

Crusty Parmesan Chicken Drumsticks

25 minutes

¼ cup Dijon mustard

4 tblspn oil

4 tblspn finely chopped spring onions (scallions)

¼ tspn ground black pepper

¼ cup freshly grated Parmesan cheese

8 chicken drumsticks

½ cup breadcrumbs

¼ cup melted butter

1 In a medium bowl, combine the mustard, oil, spring onions, pepper and Parmesan cheese, mix well.

2 Coat each chicken drumstick with the mustard cheese mixture with a pastry brush, then roll them in the breadcrumbs and coat completely.

3 Dab each drumstick with the melted butter and bake in a moderate oven for 10-12 minutes, turning them twice.

Serves 4

Sauteed Chicken Breasts In Curry Cream Sauce

20 minutes

2 tblspn butter

4 double chicken fillets, cut in half

½ cup coconut cream

1 cup cream

¼ tspn ground coriander

½ tspn ground cumin

2 tspn medium curry powder

2 tblspn chopped fresh basil

1 Melt the butter in a large frying pan over moderate heat, add chicken fillets and cook until golden on both sides, but pink inside. Transfer fillets to a baking dish and cook in a moderately low oven for 10 minutes.

2 Meanwhile, add the coconut cream, cream, coriander, cumin and curry powder and cook until sauce is reduced by half.

3 Arrange chicken fillets on a serving plate, pour curry sauce over the top and sprinkle with the basil.

Serves 4

Chicken Piccata

10 minutes

4 chicken breast halves

plain flour

4 tblspn unsalted butter

1 cup dry vermouth

½ cup chicken stock

½ cup chopped fresh parsley

salt

pepper

2 tblspn drained capers

lemon slices for garnish

1 Flatten chicken between waxed paper with a mallet. Cut into thin strips. Dredge in flour, shaking off excess.

2 Melt butter in a heavy based pan, add chicken and cook, tossing, 1-2 minutes to brown. Add vermouth, stock and parsley, season with salt and freshly ground pepper.

3 Lower heat, cook until chicken is done, about 4-6 minutes. Garnish with capers and lemon slices.

Serves 4

Chicken with Creamy Tarragon Sauce

20 minutes

3 tblspn butter

4 double chicken fillets

1 tblspn finely chopped fresh tarragon

1 tblspn Dijon mustard

¾ cup dry white wine

1 cup cream

1 Melt the butter in a large frying pan over moderate heat. Add the chicken fillets to the pan and cook for about 2 minutes or until chicken is only just cooked. Transfer fillets to a baking dish, keep warm in a very low oven.

2 Add the tarragon, mustard and wine to the pan, bring to the boil and reduce by half.

3 Add the cream and cook until mixture boils and thickens slightly, about 3 minutes. Pour sauce over chicken fillets.

Serves 4

Stir-fried Chicken with Snowpeas

12 minutes

1 tblspn vegetable oil

750g (1½lb) skinless chicken breasts, cut into bite-size pieces

salt

pepper

200g (6½oz) snowpeas, strings removed

3 tblspn finely grated fresh ginger

1 clove garlic, finely chopped

⅓ cup chicken stock

1½ tblspn soy sauce

1 bunch coriander, roughly chopped

1 Heat oil in a wok or heavy based frying pan. Sprinkle chicken with salt and freshly ground pepper and stir-fry over high heat for 4 minutes. Add snowpeas and stir-fry another 2 minutes. Add ginger and garlic, stir-fry 1 minute longer. Push all to one side of the pan.

2 Add chicken stock and soy sauce to pan and simmer 1 minute. Toss chicken and snowpeas in this stock. Sprinkle with chopped coriander and serve immediately.

Serves 4

Chicken Pieces with Apples and Onions

20 minutes

3 tblspn butter

4 double chicken fillets, cut into 2cm (¾in) squares

2 red apples, cored and sliced

1 large red onion

4 celery stalks, sliced

¼ cup freshly squeezed orange juice

¼ cup apple juice

¼ tspn cracked black pepper

1 cup cream

1 Melt the butter in a large saucepan over moderate heat. Add the chicken, apple, onion and celery, cook for 3 minutes.

2 Add the orange juice, apple juice and pepper and simmer for 5 minutes.

3 Add the cream, bring to the boil and cook for a further 5 minutes or until sauce thickens slightly.

Serves 4

Chicken Marsala

12 minutes

4 chicken fillets

3 tblspn butter

½ cup plain flour

salt

pepper

⅓ cup Marsala

2 tblspn butter, extra

3 tblspn chopped chives

1 Slice chicken fillets in half horizontally.

2 Heat butter in a heavy based frying pan until foaming. Dredge chicken in flour. Shake off excess and place in pan, cook 1 minute on each side, until golden brown. Transfer to a warm platter. Season to taste with salt and freshly ground pepper.

3 Remove all but 1 tablespoon of fat from the pan. Add Marsala, boil 1 minute, scraping up any browned bits. Add butter and any chicken juices from reserved chicken.

4 Cook until sauce thickens, reduce heat, return chicken breast to pan, baste well with the sauce and heat through. Serve immediately.

Serves 4

Stuffed Chicken Legs

40 minutes

1 clove garlic, finely chopped

250g (½lb) ricotta cheese

2 tblspn freshly grated Parmesan cheese

1 egg, lightly beaten

1 slice of day-old white bread, crumbled

2 tblspn finely chopped basil

salt

pepper

8 chicken legs

juice of 1 lemon

8 bacon slices

1 In a large bowl, mix together garlic, cheeses, egg, bread and basil. Season to taste with salt and freshly ground pepper. Stir well to combine.

2 Loosen skin of chicken leg gently and carefully stuff 1-2 tablespoons of the mixture under chicken skin, pushing upwards.

3 Sprinkle with lemon juice, cover with bacon strips. Place in a 225°C (450°F) oven, cook until juices run clear, about 25 minutes.

Serves 4

Chicken Pieces with Apples and Onions (top); Chicken with Creamy Tarragon Sauce (bottom)

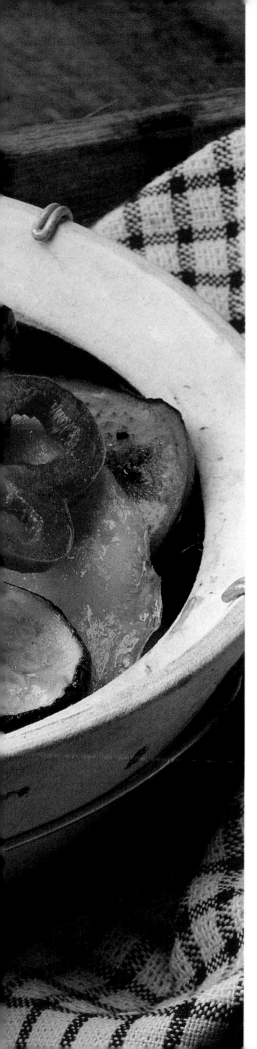

VEGETABLE ACCOMPANIMENTS

Tasty vegetable dishes can turn a plain meal into a memorable one.

Eggplant (Aubergine), Zucchini (Courgette) and Capsicum (Pepper) Bake

40 minutes

3 medium potatoes, peeled and thinly sliced

1 large eggplant (aubergine), thinly sliced

3 zucchini (courgette), thinly sliced

1 red capsicum (pepper), thinly sliced

½ tspn salt

¼ tspn ground black pepper

¼ cup melted butter

¼ cup olive oil

2 cloves garlic, crushed

1 Arrange vegetables in a baking dish, alternating each. Sprinkle with salt and pepper and pour over combined butter, oil and garlic.

2 Bake in a moderate oven for 30 minutes or until cooked.

Serves 4

Sauteed Shredded Beets with Hazelnuts

7 minutes

3 tblspn unsalted butter

3 large beets, peeled and shredded

salt

pepper

¼ cup chopped toasted hazelnuts

2 tblspn chopped parsley

1 Melt butter in a heavy non-stick frying pan. Add beets and cook, stirring, 3-4 minutes, until beginning to soften. Season to taste with salt and freshly ground pepper.

2 Place in a heated serving dish, sprinkle with nuts and parsley. Serve immediately.

Serves 6

Parsnip and Apple Pancakes

20 minutes

345g (11oz) parsnips, peeled and grated

1 large Granny Smith apple, peeled and grated

3 eggs, lightly beaten

1 tspn salt

1½ tblspn plain flour

pinch of baking powder

1½ tblspn brown sugar

2 tblspn vegetable oil

1 Mix grated parsnip and apple with the eggs, salt, flour, baking powder and brown sugar.

2 Heat oil in a heavy non-stick frying pan. Drop the batter into the oil in rounded tablespoons, flattening with an egg-slice.

3 Cook pancakes for 5 minutes on each side. Drain briefly on paper towels and serve immediately.

Serves 6

Eggplant (Aubergine), Zucchini (Courgette) and Capsicum (Pepper) Bake

Sugarpeas and Snowpeas with Yoghurt and Mint

5 minutes

250g (½lb) sugar snap peas, topped and tailed

250g (½lb) snowpeas, topped and tailed

1 cup sour cream, room temperature

¼ cup plain yoghurt, room temperature

2 tblspn chopped fresh mint

¼ tspn ground cumin

½ cup finely chopped Spanish onion

salt

pepper

1 Plunge peas in a large pot of boiling, lightly salted water; when water returns to the boil, cook 5 seconds, drain.

2 Combine sour cream, yoghurt, mint, cumin and onion in a serving bowl, stir in sugar snap peas and snowpeas. Season to taste with salt and freshly ground pepper. Serve at room temperature.

Serves 6

Stir-fry Vegetables

10 minutes

¼ cup butter

4 carrots, finely sliced

3 celery sticks, finely chopped

1 large leek, finely sliced

2 cups chopped green beans

2 tblspn finely chopped ginger

2 tblspn soy sauce

½ cup peanuts

1 bunch coriander, carefully rinsed, leaves removed and stems chopped

1 Melt butter in a wok or heavy non-stick frying pan. Add carrots, celery, leek, beans, ginger, soy sauce, peanuts and coriander stems, not the leaves.

Pommes Patricia ·

2 Stir-fry until vegetables are cooked through, but still crunchy. Serve immediately with a garnish of coriander leaves.

Serves 6

Sauteed Savoy Cabbage with Apples

15 minutes

3 tblspn mustard seed oil

2 Granny Smith apples, peeled, cored and thinly sliced

1 onion, finely sliced

1 large savoy cabbage, shredded

½ cup dry white wine

salt

pepper

1 Heat oil in a large non-stick frying pan. Add apples and onion, saute 4 minutes, or until softened. Add cabbage and saute until cabbage wilts, about 2 minutes.

2 Add wine, salt and freshly ground pepper to taste. Simmer, stirring occasionally, until cabbage is tender, about 5-6 minutes. Serve immediately.

Serves 6

Pommes Patricia

40 minutes

6 medium potatoes, peeled and cut into 2cm (¾in) cubes

2 red onions, cut into 2cm (¾in) squares

¼ cup olive oil

2 cloves garlic, crushed

3 tspn ground cumin

½ tspn ground pepper

2 tspn chopped continental parsley

1 Place the potato and onions in a greased baking tray. Pour over combined oil, garlic, cumin and pepper, cook in moderate oven for 30 minutes. Stir in parsley and serve immediately.

Serves 4

Braised Fennel with Parmesan Cheese

25 minutes

3 large heads of fennel

30g (1oz) unsalted butter

salt

pepper

1 glass white wine

60g (2oz) freshly grated Parmesan cheese

Asparagus with Orange Hollandaise

1 Remove tough outer layer of fennel. Cut each head into quarters.

2 Melt butter in a heavy shallow ovenproof dish. Toss fennel in the melted butter. Season to taste with salt and freshly ground pepper. Pour in wine and cover with a lid. Cook gently in a moderate oven for 15-20 minutes or until tender.

3 Sprinkle with Parmesan and brown for a few minutes under a grill. Serve immediately.

Serves 6

Mixed Squash with Sun-dried Tomatoes

5 minutes

6 yellow baby squash
6 green baby squash
3 small zucchini (courgette)
6 sun-dried tomatoes
3 tblspn oil from the sun-dried tomatoes
1 tblspn chopped fresh rosemary
salt
pepper

1 Cut squash and zucchini into 0.5cm (¼in) slices. Slice tomatoes into thin strips.

2 In a heavy non-stick frying pan heat oil and saute squash and zucchini on both sides until light brown. Add tomatoes and rosemary, season to taste with salt and freshly ground pepper.

3 Toss well to mix, serve immediately.

Serves 6

Herbed Cherry Tomatoes

6 minutes

60g (2oz) butter
2 tblspn lemon juice
2 tblspn finely chopped parsley
2 tblspn finely chopped basil
2 tblspn finely snipped chives
3 punnets cherry tomatoes
pepper

1 Melt butter in a heavy non-stick frying pan. Cook over low heat until butter begins to brown. Add lemon juice, parsley, chives and basil.

2 Stir in tomatoes and cook, tossing, 3-4 minutes over moderate heat, until skins begin to burst. Add freshly ground pepper to taste, serve immediately.

Serves 6

Asparagus with Orange Hollandaise

10 minutes

2 bunches fresh asparagus, trimmed
3 egg yolks
1 tblspn freshly squeezed lemon juice
3 tspn finely grated orange rind
1 tblspn freshly squeezed orange juice
125g (4oz) butter

1 Bring a large saucepan of water to the boil. Add asparagus and simmer for 2 minutes, or until asparagus is just tender, drain.

2 Combine egg yolks, lemon juice, orange rind and orange juice in a blender or food processor, blend for 10 seconds.

3 Melt the butter in a small saucepan, when butter is bubbling, immediately pour into food processor or blender, while motor is operating, in a slow steady stream.

4 Place asparagus on a serving plate, spoon sauce over the top and garnish with strips of orange rind.

Serves 4

Zucchini (Courgette) Batons with Prosciutto and Mustard Mayonnaise

10 minutes

6 medium zucchini (courgette), cut into 0.5 x 4cm (¼ x 1½in) strips

10 slices prosciutto, cut into thin strips

MAYONNAISE

2 egg yolks

1 tblspn cider vinegar

2 tspn Dijon mustard

½ cup vegetable oil

¾ cup olive oil

1 Bring a large saucepan of water to the boil over moderate heat. Add the zucchini batons and cook for 1 minute. Drain and refresh under cold water, drain again and set aside.

2 To make mayonnaise: Combine eggs, vinegar and mustard in a blender or food processor for 10 seconds. Gradually pour the oils into food processor or blender, while motor is operating, in a slow steady stream.

3 Spread the mayonnaise on a serving plate, arrange zucchini batons on top and scatter with prosciutto strips.

Serves 4

Baked Sweet Potato (Kumera) with Rosemary and Garlic

35 minutes

2 medium sweet potatoes (kumera), peeled and cut into 0.5cm (¼in) thick slices

1 tblspn finely chopped fresh rosemary

2 cloves garlic, crushed

1 tspn salt

¼ cup olive oil

1 Place the slices of sweet potato in a greased baking dish. Sprinkle with the rosemary and pour over combined garlic, salt and oil.

Zucchini (Courgette) Batons with Prosciutto and Mustard Mayonaisse (top); Baked Sweet Potato (Kumera) with Rosemary and Garlic (bottom)

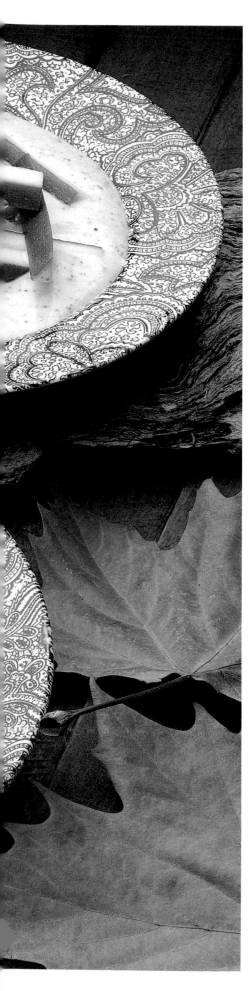

Sauteed Squash, Snowpeas and Red Capsicum (Pepper) Strips (top);
Pan-fried Vegetables with Ricotta Cheese (bottom)

2 Bake in a moderate oven for 30 minutes, stirring and turning occasionally.

Serves 4

Pan-fried Vegetables with Ricotta Cheese

10 minutes

3 tblspn butter

1 eggplant (aubergine), sliced and chopped

4 zucchini (courgettes), sliced

200g (6½oz) yellow squash, quartered

2 tblspn tarragon vinegar

300g (9½oz) ricotta cheese

1 Heat the butter in a large frying pan over moderate heat, add the eggplant, zucchini and squash, cook for 3 minutes.

2 Add the vinegar and toss vegetables, cook for a further 1 minute.

3 Spoon a small serving of ricotta cheese onto each plate and serve vegetables over the top.

Serves 4

Sauteed Squash, Snowpeas and Red Capsicum (Pepper) Strips

10 minutes

2 tblspn butter

2 red capsicum (pepper), seeded and cut into thin strips

300g (10oz) yellow squash, thinly sliced

155g (5oz) snowpeas, topped and tailed

2 tspn finely chopped fresh parsley

2 tspn finely chopped fresh basil

1 Heat the butter in a medium frying pan over moderate heat. Add the capsicum strips, and cook for 1 minute.

2 Add the squash and snowpeas, cook for a further 1 minute.

3 Stir in parsley and basil, serve immediately.

Serves 4

SIDE SALADS

These salads are easy to prepare and will provide the perfect complement to a main dish.

Italian Salad

8 minutes

8 cups shredded romaine lettuce

2 fennel bulbs, trimmed, sliced lengthwise

1 tin of marinated artichoke hearts, drained

1 small jar sun-dried tomatoes

8 tblspn marinated olives

fresh basil sprigs

freshly grated Parmesan cheese

DRESSING

6 tblspn freshly squeezed lemon juice

3 tblspn Dijon mustard

1 cup olive oil

6 anchovy fillets, finely chopped

pepper

1 To make dressing: Combine lemon juice and mustard. Gradually whisk in oil. Add anchovy fillets and freshly ground pepper.

2 Place lettuce in a bowl. Toss and coat with a little of the dressing. Divide among 6 plates.

3 Arrange fennel, artichokes, tomatoes, olives and basil over the lettuce in a decorative pattern. Drizzle with dressing. Sprinkle grated Parmesan cheese over salad. Serve immediately.

Serves 6

Fennel Salad with Pimentos

5 minutes

1 fennel bulb, white part only, finely sliced

2 red onions, peeled and finely sliced

1 cup pimentos, drained and cut into thin strips

¼ cup continental parsley leaves

¼ cup French dressing

¼ tspn cracked black pepper

1 Arrange the fennel, onion, pimentos and parsley on a serving plate.

2 Dress with combined French dressing and black pepper.

Serves 4

Fennel Salad with Pimentos

Broad Bean Salad

15 minutes

2½ cups frozen broad beans, thawed

150ml (¼ pint) plain yoghurt

3 tblspn mayonnaise

1 tblspn chopped chives

1 Bring a large saucepan of salted water to the boil, add broad beans and cook for about 7 minutes, or until tender.

2 Drain beans and mix with the yoghurt, mayonnaise and chives.

Serves 4

Avocado and Bocconcini Salad with Warm Tomato Vinaigrette

6 minutes

3 avocados

6 bocconcini

basil sprigs to garnish

DRESSING

4 large tomatoes, peeled, seeded, diced

1 cup chopped basil leaves

8 tblspn red wine vinegar

1 cup light olive oil

3 tblspn Dijon mustard

salt

pepper

1 To make dressing: Combine tomatoes, basil, vinegar, oil and mustard in a saucepan. Bring slowly to a simmer, season to taste with salt and freshly ground pepper.

2 Cut bocconcini and avocado into thin slices. Arrange on a platter in alternate slices. Spoon warm dressing over and garnish with basil sprigs.

Serves 6

Broccoli and Cauliflower Salad

10 minutes

500g (1lb) broccoli flowerets

500g (1lb) cauliflowerets

¾ cup cornichons (see note)

½ punnet cherry tomatoes

DRESSING

2 tblspn freshly squeezed orange juice

1½ tblspn Dijon mustard

½ tspn dried tarragon

½ cup olive oil

salt

pepper

1 Steam broccoli and cauliflower for 3 minutes. Rinse under cold water and drain well. Combine with cornichons and tomatoes in a large bowl.

2 To make dressing: Combine orange juice, mustard and tarragon. Gradually whisk in oil, season to taste with salt and freshly ground pepper.

3 Pour dressing over vegetables, toss well to coat. Serve immediately or refrigerate for up to 2 hours.
Note: Cornichons are miniature gherkins, available at delicatessens and major food halls.

Serves 6

Watercress Salad with Pears and Radishes

10 minutes

3 cups watercress sprigs

1 pear, cut into thin slices

½ cup finely sliced radishes

3 tblspn apple juice

1 tblspn lemon juice

1 tspn lemon rind

2 tblspn olive oil

1 Arrange the watercress, pear slices and radish slices in serving bowl, toss well.

2 Pour over combined apple juice, lemon juice, lemon rind and olive oil and serve immediately.

Serves 4

Orange and Fennel Salad

6 minutes

1kg (2lb) fennel bulbs, cut into thin slices

6 navel oranges, peeled and thinly sliced

6 tblspn continental parsley, roughly chopped

DRESSING

1½ tblspn balsamic vinegar

¼ tspn salt

3 tblspn extra virgin olive oil

1 Arrange alternate slices of fennel and orange on a platter, top with chopped parsley.

2 To make dressing: Whisk together vinegar and salt. Gradually whisk in oil.

3 Drizzle dressing over salad, serve immediately.

Serves 6

Broad Bean Salad (top);
Watercress Salad with Pears and
Radishes (bottom)

Two Pea Salad

5 minutes

375g (¾lb) snowpeas, topped and tailed

375g (¾lb) sugar snap peas, topped and tailed

DRESSING

1½ tblspn vegetable oil

1½ tblspn sesame seeds

1½ tblspn white wine vinegar

2½ tspn sugar

1 tspn soy sauce

1 To make dressing: Heat oil over moderate heat. Add sesame seeds and cook until light brown, about 3 minutes. Remove from heat, stir in vinegar, sugar and soy sauce.

2 Bring very lightly salted water to a boil in a saucepan. Add snow and sugar peas, cook 1 minute. Rinse under cold water and drain well.

3 Combine peas with sesame seed dressing, toss well to coat. Serve immediately.

Serves 6

Mustard Potatoes

50 minutes — includes chilling time

1kg (2lb) baby potatoes, washed and boiled

¼ cup sour cream

¼ cup mayonnaise

2 tblspn grainy mustard

2 tblspn French dressing

1 Chill potatoes before serving.

2 Mix together the sour cream, mayonnaise, mustard and French dressing and spoon over the potatoes.

Serves 4

Mustard Potatoes

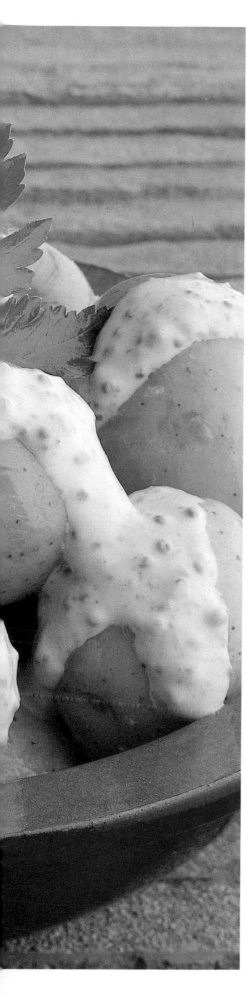

Two Bean Salad

Two Bean Salad

15 minutes

2 cups green beans, trimmed and cut into 2cm (¾in) lengths

1 cup canned dark red kidney beans, rinsed

½ red capsicum (pepper), seeded and cut into very thin strips

rind and juice of 1 orange, rind cut into very thin strips

2 tblspn red wine vinegar

3 tblspn olive oil

¼ tspn cracked black pepper

2 tspn finely chopped fresh tarragon

1 Cook the green beans in a large saucepan of boiling water until crisp-tender, about 3 minutes, drain and refresh under cold water.

2 Combine green beans with the kidney beans, capsicum and rind.

3 Pour over combined orange juice, vinegar, oil, pepper and tarragon and toss well.

Serves 4

Coriander, Mushroom and Tomato Salad

10 minutes

2 bunches fresh coriander, washed carefully, roughly chopped

375g (¾lb) button mushrooms, sliced

2 punnets cherry tomatoes, halved

DRESSING

3 tspn Dijon mustard

4½ tspn red wine vinegar

6 tblspn olive oil

salt

pepper

1 Combine coriander, mushrooms and tomatoes in a salad bowl.

2 To make dressing: Combine mustard and vinegar in a small bowl. Gradually whisk in oil, season to taste with salt and freshly ground pepper.

3 Pour dressing over salad, toss to coat. Serve immediately.

Serves 6

Spinach and Bacon Salad with Blue Vein Dressing

Red Cabbage Salad with Goat's Cheese

12 minutes

2 cups red cabbage, finely sliced

1 tblspn olive oil

½ cup finely chopped bacon, rind removed

¼ cup red wine vinegar

2 tblspn chopped chives

¾ cup goat's cheese, crumbled

1 Arrange cabbage in serving bowl.

2 Heat the oil in a large frying pan over moderate heat, add the bacon and cook until crispy. Remove bacon from pan and set aside.

3 Add vinegar to pan and cook for 1 minute, set aside.

4 Sprinkle bacon, chives and cheese over cabbage and dress with the reserved red wine vinegar dressing.

Serves 4

Spinach and Bacon Salad with Blue Vein Dressing

15 minutes

1 tblspn olive oil

½ cup finely chopped bacon

¾ cup slivered almonds

3 cups roughly chopped spinach

2 tblspn blue vein cheese, crumbled

1 tblspn mayonnaise

1 tblspn sour cream

¼ cup cream

1 Heat the oil in a large frying pan over moderate heat, add the bacon and cook until crispy. Add the almonds to the pan and cook until golden, about 3 minutes.

2 Arrange the spinach on a serving plate, add the bacon and almonds, toss salad.

3 In a small bowl, combine the cheese with the mayonnaise, sour cream and cream, mix well. Pour dressing over salad just before serving.

Serves 4

Warm Butter Lettuce and Endive Salad

6 minutes

1 butter lettuce, torn into bite-size pieces

1 bunch curly endive, torn into bite-size pieces

5 bacon rashers, trimmed and cut into 4cm (1½in) pieces

2 tblspn oil

250g (½lb) button mushrooms, thinly sliced

1 red capsicum (pepper), seeded and julienned

1 small onion, thinly sliced

1 tspn Worcestershire sauce

2 tblspn chopped fresh dill

salt

pepper

¼ cup balsamic vinegar

1 tblspn butter, room temperature

1 Place butter lettuce and endive in a large bowl.

2 Cook bacon in a heavy non-stick frying pan until crisp. Remove with a slotted spoon. Drain on paper towels, add to lettuce. Pour off all but 2 tablespoons fat from the pan. Set aside.

3 Heat oil in a heavy non-stick frying pan. Add mushrooms, capsicum and onion. Stir until heated through. Add Worcestershire sauce and dill. Season with salt and freshly ground pepper. Add to greens.

4 Add vinegar to reserved bacon fat. Bring to a boil, scraping up any browned bits. Add butter and stir until melted. Pour over salad and toss well. Serve immediately.

Serves 6

Red Cabbage Salad with Goat's Cheese

PASTA TO PLEASE

Pasta is perfect for quick meals as it cooks in just a few minutes and can be served with a variety of sauces.

Penne with Bacon and Walnuts

20 minutes

500g (1lb) penne pasta

3 tblspn olive oil

2 cloves garlic, crushed

6 bacon rashers, finely chopped, rind removed

2 tblspn chopped fresh basil

¼ tspn cracked black pepper

½ cup roughly chopped walnuts

¼ cup freshly grated Parmesan cheese

1 Bring a large saucepan of water to the boil, add the pasta and cook until just tender, drain.

2 Meanwhile heat the oil in a large frying pan over moderate heat. Add the garlic, cook for 1 minute. Add the bacon and cook for a further 2 minutes. Add the basil, pepper and walnuts and heat through.

3 Toss pasta with bacon and walnuts and serve immediately. Top with fresh Parmesan cheese.

Serves 4

Ravioli with Mushrooms and Sugar Snap Peas

20 minutes

500g (1lb) ravioli

30g (1oz) butter

2 cloves garlic, crushed

2 cups button mushrooms, halved

1 cup sugar snap peas, trimmed and cut into 1cm (½in) lengths

½ cup cherry tomatoes, quartered

1 tblspn olive oil

¼ cup freshly grated Parmesan cheese

1 Bring a large saucepan of water to the boil, add ravioli and cook until tender, about 12-15 minutes, drain, set aside.

2 Melt the butter in a large frying pan over moderate heat, add the garlic and mushrooms, cook for 2 minutes. Add the peas, tomatoes and oil and cook for a further 2 minutes. Mix in the cheese, combine with ravioli and serve immediately.

Serves 4

Penne with Bacon and Walnuts (top); Ravioli with Mushrooms and Sugar Snap Peas (bottom)

Macaroni with Ham, Cheese and Tomato

45 minutes

250g (½lb) macaroni

salt

2 tspn unsalted butter

1 onion, chopped

250g (½lb) mild ham steaks, cut into 1cm (½in) cubes

2 tblspn unsalted butter, extra

2 tblspn plain flour

450ml (¾pint) milk

185g (6oz) mature Cheddar cheese, grated

60g (2oz) Parmesan cheese, grated

1 tblspn Dijon mustard

pepper

2 tomatoes, sliced

¼ cup fresh breadcrumbs

2 tblspn unsalted butter, extra, cut into pea-size cubes

1 Cook macaroni in salted boiling water until al dente.

2 Meanwhile, melt butter in a non-stick frying pan, add onion, cook until golden, about 5 minutes. Add ham, saute a further 5 minutes, reserve.

3 In the meantime, in a small saucepan melt extra butter, whisk in flour until smooth, cook over gentle heat for 2 minutes. Off the heat, pour in milk all at once, stir until smooth. Return to the heat, stir until sauce thickens.

4 Add Cheddar and half of the Parmesan cheese, stir off the heat until cheese is melted. Stir in mustard and freshly ground pepper. Add reserved ham and onion mixture, stir in well.

5 Drain macaroni, place in an ovenproof dish, brushed with butter. Pour sauce over macaroni, mix in well. Arrange tomato slices on top, scatter with breadcrumbs, then with remaining Parmesan. Top with butter cubes.

Fettucine with Creamy Smoked Salmon Sauce

6 Bake in a 200°C (400°F) oven until dish is heated through and top is golden and crispy. Serve hot.

Serves 4

Spaghetti Carbonara

20 minutes

500g (1lb) spaghetti

salt

2 tblspn olive oil

155g (5oz) rolled, sliced pancetta or bacon, cut into strips

1 clove garlic, finely chopped

¼ tspn chilli flakes (optional)

4 eggs

¼ cup freshly grated Parmesan cheese

pepper

freshly grated Parmesan cheese, extra

1 Cook spaghetti in lightly salted boiling water until al dente.

2 Meanwhile, combine oil, pancetta or bacon, garlic and chilli flakes, if used, in a small frying pan. Heat very gently, until pancetta is golden.

3 While pancetta is heating, combine eggs and Parmesan cheese in a bowl. Beat until well combined.

4 Drain pasta, place in a large, heated bowl. Quickly pour over the hot oil and pancetta mixture, then the egg and cheese. Toss thoroughly to coat. The hot pasta will 'cook' the eggs. Season with freshly ground pepper. Serve hot with Parmesan cheese separately.

Serves 4

Tortellini with Butter

Fettucine with Creamy Smoked Salmon Sauce

20 minutes

500g (1lb) fettucine

1 cup fresh peas

3 tblspn sweet white wine

1 cup cream

8 slices smoked salmon

3 tblspn cream, extra

1 tblspn finely chopped spring onions (scallions)

1 Bring a large saucepan of water to the boil over moderate heat. Add the fettucine and cook until just tender.

2 Meanwhile, blanch the peas in a saucepan of boiling water for 2 minutes, remove with a slotted spoon and refresh under cold water, drain and set aside.

3 Bring the wine to a boil in a large frying pan, add the cream and cook over high heat until sauce thickens, set aside.

4 In a blender or food processor, puree 4 slices of smoked salmon, extra cream and spring onions, pour mixture into frying pan and mix with cream sauce over moderate heat until hot.

5 Cut the remaining 4 slices of salmon into strips and add to the sauce, stir in peas.

6 Drain pasta and pour over sauce, toss well, serve immediately.

Serves 4

Tortellini with Butter

15 minutes

2 tblspn olive oil

500g (1lb) tortellini

1 cup freshly grated Parmesan cheese

125g (4oz) butter, cut into small cubes

¼ tspn ground nutmeg

¼ cup chopped fresh parsley

1 Bring a large saucepan of water to the boil over moderate heat. Add the olive oil and tortellini, cook until the tortellini begin to float to the surface and are cooked through, drain.

2 Place the tortellini in a large serving bowl and toss with the Parmesan cheese, butter, nutmeg and parsley. Serve immediately.

Serves 4

Fried Rice

25 minutes

⅓ cup peanut oil

1 Spanish onion, chopped

1 stalk celery, thinly sliced

1 red capsicum (pepper), seeded, chopped

2 cups chopped cooked chicken

4 cups cooked rice

227g (7oz) can water chestnuts, drained, quartered

2 eggs, lightly beaten

soy sauce

1 Heat oil in a large frying pan over moderately high heat. Add onion, cook until golden, about 5 minutes. Add celery and capsicum, cook until crisp-tender, about 3 minutes.

2 Add chicken, rice and water chestnuts, heat through, stirring constantly.

3 Add eggs, stir-fry until well incorporated. Cook until heated through, about 4 minutes. Season to taste with soy sauce. Serve hot.

Serves 4

Risotto with Smoked Salmon (above); Chilli Con Carne (right)

Risotto with Smoked Salmon

30 minutes

3 tblspn olive oil

2 onions, chopped

2 cloves garlic, crushed

¼ tspn turmeric

1½ cups short grain rice

1 red capsicum (pepper), seeded and chopped

3 cups fish or chicken stock

2 tblspn chopped spring onions (scallions)

1 tblspn chopped basil

1 tblspn chopped chives

8 slices smoked salmon, cut into strips

1 Heat the oil in a large frying pan over moderate heat. Add the onion, garlic and turmeric, cook for 2 minutes.

2 Add the rice and capsicum, cook for a further 2 minutes. Add the stock, simmer uncovered for 20 minutes or until rice is cooked.

3 Stir in the spring onions, basil, chives and salmon. Serve hot or cold.

Serves 4

Bulgur, Rice and Barley Pilaf

40 minutes

2 tblspn unsalted butter

1 onion, chopped

1 clove garlic, crushed

1½ cups chicken stock, or same amount of water with stock cubes

¼ cup bulgur

¼ cup long-grain rice

¼ cup pearl barley

Tabasco sauce

¼ cup coarsely chopped continental parsley

2 tblspn chopped fresh chives

1 Melt butter in a large frying pan over medium heat. Add onion and garlic, cook until golden, about 5 minutes.

2 Add chicken stock, bulgur, rice and barley. Season to taste with Tabasco. Bring to a boil, reduce heat, cover. Simmer until all liquid has been absorbed, about 30 minutes.

3 Stir in parsley and chives. Serve hot.

Serves 4

Chilli Con Carne

25 minutes

2 tblspn olive oil

2 medium onions, chopped

2 cloves garlic, crushed

¼ tspn chilli powder

500g (1lb) lean minced beef

3 tblspn tomato paste

¼ cup red wine

1 cup chopped tinned tomatoes

1½ cups rinsed and drained canned red kidney beans

1 cup grated mature cheese

½ cup sour cream

1 Heat the oil in a large frying pan over moderate heat. Add the onion, garlic and chilli powder, cook for 2 minutes.

2 Stir in mince, cook a further 5 minutes.

3 Stir in tomato paste, wine, tomatoes and beans, simmer for 10 minutes.

4 Pour into 4 warmed bowls, top with cheese and sour cream.

Serves 4

Fettucine with Creamy Pumpkin Sauce

20 minutes

500g (1lb) fettucine

2 cups thickened cream

¾ cup cooked mashed pumpkin

¼ tspn ground black pepper

½ tspn ground nutmeg

1 tspn chopped chives

1 cup pumpkin, cut into strips, blanched

1 Bring a large saucepan of water to the boil, add fettucine and cook until just tender. Drain.

2 Meanwhile heat the cream in a large deep frying pan until reduced by half.

3 Whisk in the mashed pumpkin, pepper and nutmeg, gently stir in the chives and pumpkin strips.

4 Stir in the fettucine and toss gently. Serve immediately.

Serves 4

Bacon and Bean Bake

40 minutes

250g (½lb) bacon rashers

1 onion, chopped

½ cup tomato ketchup

¼ cup firmly packed brown sugar

1 tblspn red wine vinegar

1 tblspn Dijon mustard

310g (10oz) can red kidney beans, drained

310g (10oz) can lima beans, drained

310g (10oz) can butter beans, drained

1 Cook bacon in a frying pan until golden and crisp, about 5 minutes. Remove with a slotted spoon to paper towels. Reserve fat in the pan.

2 Add onion to frying pan, cook until golden, about 5 minutes. Pour onions and bacon fat into a large bowl.

Fettucine with Creamy Pumpkin Sauce

3 Add ketchup, sugar, vinegar and mustard to the bowl, mix well. Crumble bacon, add to bowl. Mix in drained beans, transfer mixture to an ovenproof serving dish.

4 Bake in a 180°C (350°F) oven until beans are heated through and bubbly, about 30 minutes. Serve hot.

Serves 4-6

Pasta Primavera

25 minutes

salt

½ cup broccoli flowerets

½ cup cauliflowerets

1 zucchini (courgette), thinly sliced

1 small carrot, cut diagonally into thin slices

500g (1lb) thin spaghetti

1 tblspn olive oil

2 spring onions (scallions), thinly sliced

1 small tomato, chopped

½ green capsicum (pepper), chopped

1 small jar prepared pesto sauce

125g (4oz) prosciutto, cut into thin strips

Parmesan cheese to serve

1 Bring 1 medium and 1 large saucepan of lightly salted water to a boil.

2 Plunge broccoli, cauliflower, zucchini and carrot into medium pan of boiling water. Allow water to return to a boil, cook vegetables for 2 minutes, drain. Add spaghetti to boiling water in the large saucepan, cook until al dente (cooked but firm).

3 Meanwhile, heat oil in a frying pan, add drained vegetables and spring onions, tomato and capsicum. Stir-fry for 4 minutes, or until vegetables are crisp-tender.

4 Drain pasta, place in a large, heated bowl. Add vegetables, pesto and prosciutto, toss well to mix. Serve immediately with Parmesan cheese in a separate bowl.

Serves 4

Fettucine with Scallops and Red Capsicum (Pepper)

20 minutes

500g (1lb) fettucine

30g (1oz) butter

1 red capsicum (pepper), seeded, cut into strips

2 tblspn chopped spring onions (scallions)

1½ cups cream

500g (1lb) scallops, deveined

½ tspn ground black pepper

1 tblspn chopped fresh parsley

1 Bring a large saucepan of water to the boil over moderate heat. Add the fettucine and cook until just tender.

2 Meanwhile, melt the butter in a large frying pan over moderate heat. Add the capsicum strips and spring onions, cook for 1 minute.

3 Add the cream, bring to the boil, reduce heat and simmer for 3-5 minutes, or until cream begins to thicken.

4 Add the scallops and pepper, cook until the scallops are opaque, about 1 minute. Drain fettucine and pour scallop sauce over the top, sprinkle with parsley.

Serves 4

Penne with Mussels in Orange Cream Sauce

35 minutes

salt

500g (1lb) penne

⅓ cup unsalted butter

8 spring onions (scallions), chopped

6 strips orange zest

¼ tspn fennel seeds

2kg (4lb) mussels, scrubbed and debearded

1 cup cream

pepper

1 Bring a large saucepan of lightly salted water to a boil, add penne, cook until al dente.

Fettucine with Scallops and Red Capsicum (Pepper)

2 Meanwhile, melt butter in a heavy based saucepan over medium heat. Add spring onions, cook 2 minutes. Add orange zest, fennel seeds and mussels. Cover, cook 5 minutes, remove opened mussels. Cook a further 3 minutes, remove remaining opened mussels. Discard any mussels that have not opened.

3 Remove mussels from shells, set aside. Reserve a few shells for garnish, if desired.

4 Add cream to the pan, boil until sauce thickens. Season to taste with salt and freshly ground pepper. Reduce heat, return mussels to sauce, heat through very gently.

5 Drain penne thoroughly, place in a large, heated bowl. Remove orange strips from sauce, pour sauce over penne. Toss well to mix. Serve hot, garnished with reserved mussel shells.

Serves 4

Spaghetti with Red Capsicum (Pepper) and Prosciutto

20 minutes

2 red capsicum (peppers)

salt

500g (1lb) spaghetti

125g (4oz) prosciutto, not too thinly sliced

125g (4oz) mozzarella, cut into 0.5cm (¼in) cubes

3 tblspn peanut oil

3 tblspn olive oil

2 cloves garlic, finely chopped

¼ tspn chilli flakes

⅓ cup chopped continental parsley

pepper

freshly grated Parmesan cheese

Nasi Goreng

1 Plunge capsicum into plenty of boiling water. When water returns to a boil, cook 2 minutes. Remove capsicum with a slotted spoon. When slightly cooled, remove skin and seeds, cut into long thin strips. Place in a large serving bowl.

2 Add a little salt to the boiling water, add spaghetti, cook until al dente.

3 Meanwhile, add prosciutto, mozzarella, peanut and olive oils, garlic, chilli flakes and parsley to the serving bowl containing capsicum. Mix well.

4 Drain pasta, add to bowl, toss well to mix and coat. Season with freshly ground pepper. Serve hot with Parmesan cheese separately.

Serves 4

Nasi Goreng

20 minutes

2 tblspn butter

3 eggs, beaten

3 tblspn olive oil

6 bacon rashers, rind removed, chopped

1 clove garlic, crushed

2 cups peeled, deveined green prawns (uncooked shrimp) and cut into 1cm (½in) lengths

1 onion, chopped

2 tblspn soy sauce

4 cups boiled long grain rice

¼ cup chopped cucumber

3 tblspn sultanas

2 tblspn chopped fresh parsley

1 Heat the butter in a medium frying pan over moderate heat. Pour in beaten eggs, tilting pan to spread mixture evenly. Cook until underside is lightly browned, transfer to a plate and set aside.

2 Add the oil to the frying pan and heat over moderate heat, add the bacon, garlic, prawns and onion, cook for 3 minutes, remove with slotted spoon and set aside.

3 Add soy sauce, rice, cucumber and sultanas to the pan, cook 2 minutes.

4 Roll up omelette, cut into thin strips and add to frying pan. Stir in parsley, serve immediately.

Serves 4

Fettucine with Smoked Trout and Caviar

25 minutes

125g (4oz) smoked trout

salt

500g (1lb) fettucine

150ml (¼ pint) cream

1 small jar red caviar

2 tblspn chopped continental parsley for garnish

1 Remove skin and bones from trout, flake flesh.

2 Bring a large pot of lightly salted water to a boil, add fettucine and cook until al dente.

3 Meanwhile, heat cream over medium heat until slightly reduced. Add flaked trout, heat through over gentle heat for 1 minute.

4 Drain pasta, combine with cream and trout, toss well. Spoon onto heated plates, place spoonfuls of caviar on top. Serve immediately, garnished with parsley.

Serves 4

Spinach Pasta with Blue Cheese Sauce

20 minutes

salt

500g (1lb) spinach pasta

1 cup crumbled blue vein cheese

½ cup sour cream

½ cup mayonnaise

1 clove garlic, crushed

1 Bring a large saucepan of lightly salted water to a boil, add pasta, cook until al dente.

2 Meanwhile, combine cheese, sour cream, mayonnaise and garlic in a saucepan, warm gently over low heat, stirring constantly.

3 Drain pasta, place in a heated serving bowl. Pour sauce over pasta, toss well to mix and coat. Serve immediately.

Serves 4

Mushroom Risotto with Italian Sausage Bolognese

35 minutes

50g (1¾oz) butter

1 onion, finely chopped

2 cups chopped mushrooms

2 cloves garlic, crushed

1 cup short grain rice

2½ cups chicken stock

1 tblspn olive oil

1 onion, extra, finely chopped

4 Italian sausages, casings removed

¾ cup tomato puree

1 cup tinned tomatoes, chopped

1 tblspn chopped fresh basil

1 Melt the butter in a large frying pan over moderate heat. Add the onion and mushrooms, cook for 2 minutes. Add the garlic and rice, cook for a further 2 minutes.

2 Stir in the stock, bring to the boil, reduce heat, simmer uncovered for 15 minutes, stirring occasionally.

Mushroom Risotto with Italian Sausage Bolognese (left); Vermicelli with Broccoli and Almonds (below)

1 Blanch the broccoli in a medium saucepan of boiling water for 2 minutes. Drain, refresh under cold water, drain again and set aside.

2 Melt the butter in a large frying pan over moderate heat and add the spring onions, garlic, sambal oelek, pepper and almonds, cook for 2 minutes. Add the wine and oil, cook for a further 3 minutes, then add the blanched broccoli and heat through.

3 Cook the vermicelli in a large saucepan of boiling water for 30 seconds or until al dente, drain and toss with the broccoli mixture.

Serves 4

Fettucine with Creamy Avocado Sauce

20 minutes

500g (1lb) fettucine
salt
2 cloves garlic
2 ripe avocados, peeled, stoned
1 tblspn freshly squeezed lemon juice
½ cup roughly chopped fresh basil
½ cup water
pepper
2 tblspn unsalted butter
1 cup cream

1 Cook fettucine in salted boiling water until al dente.

2 Meanwhile, drop garlic through feed tube of a processor while machine is running, mince finely. Add avocado, lemon juice, basil and water. Puree, stopping at least once to scrape down sides. Season to taste with salt and freshly ground pepper.

3 Melt butter in a heavy saucepan over medium low heat, add avocado mixture, heat through, stirring constantly. Add cream, cook until sauce thickens, about 3 minutes. Check seasoning.

4 Divide pasta among 4 heated plates, pour sauce over, serve immediately.

Serves 4

3 Meanwhile, heat the oil in a large saucepan over moderate heat, add the extra onion and sausage meat, cook for 7 minutes. Add the tomato puree, tinned tomatoes and basil, simmer for a further 7 minutes.

4 Spoon risotto onto a serving plate and top with the bolognese.

Serves 4

Vermicelli with Broccoli and Almonds

15 minutes

2 cups broccoli flowerets
4 tblspn butter
2 tblspn chopped spring onions (scallions)
2 cloves garlic, crushed
1 tspn sambal oelek (chilli paste)
½ tspn cracked black pepper
½ cup chopped blanched almonds
3 tblspn white wine
3 tblspn olive oil
500g (1lb) vermicelli noodles

QUICK AND EASY SANDWICHES

Whether they're for school, work or lunch at home, these sandwiches are simple yet tasty.

Pimento and Ricotta Cheese Open Sandwiches

5 minutes

250g (½lb) ricotta cheese

½ cup Parmesan cheese, grated

1 tblspn chopped chives

4 thick slices of wholemeal bread

4 slices of pimento, drained

1 red onion, thinly sliced

parsley to garnish

1 In a small bowl, combine ricotta cheese, Parmesan cheese and chives, mix well.

2 Spread each slice of bread with the ricotta cheese mixture, top with pimento and onion rings, garnish with parsley sprigs.

Serves 4

Sauerkraut and Corned Beef Puffed Sandwiches

10 minutes

90g (3oz) Emmental cheese

1 small onion, quartered

5 tblspn mayonnaise

1 tspn Dijon mustard

pepper

1 cup sauerkraut, rinsed, thoroughly drained

4 large slices rye bread

Dijon mustard, extra, to spread

250g (8oz) thinly sliced corned beef

1 Combine cheese and onion in a processor, chop finely. Add mayonnaise, mustard and freshly ground pepper, process until well combined. Add sauerkraut, process just long enough to mix in well.

2 Place bread slices on a flat surface, spread with mustard. Drape corned beef on top, then spread with cheese and sauerkraut mixture.

3 Cook under a pre-heated griller until top is golden and puffed. Serve immediately.

Serves 4

Chicken and Avocado Open Sandwiches

10 minutes

4 slices bread

50g (1¾oz) cream cheese, softened

4 tblspn mayonnaise

2 cups cooked chicken

4 slices mature cheese

1 avocado, peeled, seeded and quartered

1 tblspn chopped chives

1 Spread each slice of bread with the cream cheese, then the mayonnaise. Top with the chicken and a slice of cheese and grill until cheese has melted.

2 Remove from grill, place avocado on top and sprinkle with chives.

Serves 4

Pimento and Ricotta Cheese Open Sandwiches (top); Chicken and Avocado Open Sandwiches (bottom)

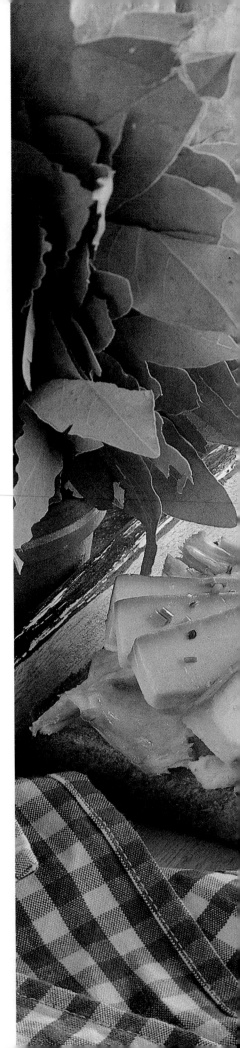

Smoked Turkey and Stilton Open Sandwiches

Double Smoked Ham Sandwiches with Gruyere and Fried Onion

16 minutes

3 tblspn unsalted butter, room temperature

1 large Spanish onion, thinly sliced

8 thin slices Italian bread

8 thin slices Gruyere cheese

8 slices double smoked ham

pepper

1 Melt 1 tablespoon of the butter in a heavy based, non-stick frying pan. Add onion, saute until softened, about 5 minutes. Set aside.

2 Use remaining butter to spread on bread, one side only. Place 4 pieces, buttered side down, on a flat surface. Top each with 1 slice of cheese and 2 slices of ham.

3 Place the fried onion on top of the ham, season with freshly ground pepper. Top with remaining cheese and place remaining slices of bread on top, buttered side up.

4 Cook sandwiches under a pre-heated griller under medium-high heat, until cheese has melted and sandwiches are golden, about 6 minutes, turning once. Serve immediately.

Serves 4

Smoked Turkey and Stilton Open Sandwiches

5 minutes

12 thick slices French bread, buttered

2 tblspn Dijon mustard

12 slices smoked turkey

200g (6½oz) Stilton cheese

watercress for garnish

1 Spread mustard on each slice of buttered bread and top with slice of turkey and crumbled Stilton. Garnish with watercress sprig.
Serves 4

Fried Mozzarella and Prosciutto Sandwiches

12 minutes

250g (½lb) mozzarella, shredded

125g (4oz) ricotta cheese

125g (4oz) prosciutto, cut into thin strips

1 tomato, seeded, chopped

1 egg, beaten

salt

pepper

12 slices bread

2 tblspn unsalted butter

2 tblspn olive oil

1 Combine mozzarella, ricotta, prosciutto, tomato and egg in a bowl. Mix well. Season to taste with salt and freshly ground pepper.

2 Spread mixture onto 6 bread slices, top with remaining bread.

118

Smoked Salmon and Egg Open Sandwiches

3 Heat butter and oil in a large frying pan over medium heat. Add sandwiches in batches, fry until golden and cheese has melted, about 2 minutes each side. Serve hot.

Makes 6

Baguette with Curly Endive and Chicken

20 minutes

1/3 cup mayonnaise

1/3 cup mango chutney

1 baguette, ends cut off, halved, halves split horizontally

FILLING

1 tblspn unsalted butter

2 chicken fillets

salt

pepper

4 cups curly endive, coarse stems discarded, rinsed and dried

1 In a small bowl combine mayonnaise with chutney, stir well until smooth. Spread a little on cut sides of bread, grill bread until golden.

2 Heat butter in a heavy based frying pan, season chicken with salt and freshly ground pepper. Add chicken to pan, saute over medium heat until cooked through, about 10 minutes, turning once. Remove chicken to a heated plate.

3 Add endive to the frying pan, season with salt and freshly ground pepper. Saute until endive just starts to wilt, about 1-2 minutes. Arrange on 2 bottom pieces of baguette.

4 Slice chicken thinly diagonally, place on top of endive. Spread with remaining mayonnaise mixture. Top with baguette, serve immediately.

Serves 2

Smoked Salmon and Egg Open Sandwiches

10 minutes

60g (2oz) butter

8 eggs

1/4 cup cream

1 tblspn chopped chives

4 slices bread

butter, extra, for spreading

4 slices smoked salmon

1 Melt the butter in a medium saucepan over moderate heat. Using a fork, mix together eggs, cream and chives until well combined. Pour mixture into saucepan and cook for 2-3 minutes stirring occasionally, or until eggs are scrambled.

2 Butter each slice of bread and lay a slice of smoked salmon on each, top with the scrambled eggs.

Makes 4

DASHING DESSERTS

End your meal with any one of these delicious desserts, all of which are quick and simple to make.

Wild Blueberry Brulee

35 minutes

2 x 450g (14½oz) cans wild blueberries, drained

6 egg yolks

¾ cup sugar

2½ cups thickened cream

1½ tblspn cold butter, cut into tiny cubes

2 tblspn castor sugar, extra

1 Divide the drained blueberries between 4 heat-proof dishes and set aside.

2 Whisk the egg yolks and sugar in the top of a double saucepan over simmering water until thick and fluffy, about 7 minutes.

3 Pour the cream into the egg sugar mixture, whisking constantly until mixture is thick enough to coat the back of a spoon, about 10 minutes. Remove from the heat and whisk in the butter.

4 Pour custard over the blueberries and chill for 10 minutes. Just before serving, sprinkle the extra sugar over the creme brulee and place each dish under a moderate grill to caramelize, about 1 minute.

Serves 4

Cherry Cobbler

25 minutes

2 x 425g (13½oz) cans stoneless black cherries, drained

⅓ cup brown sugar

1 tspn ground cinnamon

¼ cup plain flour

PASTRY

1 cup plain flour

¼ cup sugar

¼ tspn salt

2 tblspn solid vegetable shortening, frozen

1 tblspn unsalted butter, frozen

⅓ cup milk

1 Combine drained cherries, sugar, cinnamon and flour in a 20cm (8in) square baking dish.

2 To make pastry: Combine flour, sugar, baking powder, salt, shortening and butter in a processor, process until mixture resembles coarse breadcrumbs. With machine running, add milk. Process until mixture forms a ball. Place on a lightly floured surface, roll out into a 20cm (8in) square.

3 Place pastry over cherries, bake in a 225°C (450°F) oven until crust is golden brown, about 15 minutes. Serve warm.

Serves 4-6

Wild Blueberry Brulee

Rhubarb Gratin

30 minutes

8 cups fresh rhubarb, cut into 2.5cm (1in) pieces

½ cup plain sugar

¼ cup brown sugar

1 tspn ground cinnamon

3 tblspn unsalted butter, cut into pea-size pieces

⅓ cup cream

1 Place rhubarb in a buttered baking dish. Sprinkle with combined sugars and cinnamon, dot with butter. Bake in a 190°C (375°F) oven for 20 minutes.

2 Pour cream around rhubarb, bake a further 5 minutes, or until cream bubbles and rhubarb starts to become brown in places. Serve hot.

Serves 4

Apple and Pear Pie

50 minutes

1 block frozen shortcrust pastry, thawed

2 x 425g (13½oz) cans pie apples

2 x 425g (13½oz) cans pears, drained

2 tblspn freshly squeezed lemon juice

3 tblspn brown sugar

1 tspn ground cloves

1 tspn ground mixed spice

1 egg yolk

1 Roll out dough to fit the base of a 23cm (9in) removeable base flan tin, and roll out a 23cm (9in) circle for the top. Fit the base pastry circle into flan tin and bake blind for 10 minutes in a moderately hot oven.

2 In a large bowl, combine the pie apples and pears with the lemon juice, sugar, cloves and the spice.

3 Fill the crust with the apple and pear mixture and top with the second circle of pastry, pinching the edges with the crust. Brush the top of pastry with the egg yolk and pierce several times with a skewer.

Apple and Pear Pie (above); Tangy Mango Whip (left top); Mixed Berry Mousse (left bottom)

4 Bake in a moderately hot oven for 10 minutes, reduce heat to moderate and bake for a further 20 minutes.

Serves 4

Tangy Mango Whip

5 minutes

1 cup mango pulp

2 tblspn freshly squeezed lime juice

2 tblspn castor sugar

2 cups natural yoghurt

1 Puree the mango pulp, lime juice and sugar in a blender or food processor until smooth.

2 Stir in the yoghurt and pour into serving glasses. Garnish with a strawberry if desired.

Serves 4

Mixed Berry Mousse

10 minutes

2 cups mixed berries

2 tblspn red wine or port

3 tblspn castor sugar

1½ cups thickened cream

1 Place berries, (reserve ¼ cup for garnish) wine and sugar in a food processor or blender and process for 30 seconds, or until berries are just chopped.

2 Beat cream with an electric mixer until soft peaks form. Fold the berry mixture into the whipped cream, combine well.

3 Place a few of the reserved berries in the bottom of each serving glass and spoon mousse on top. Garnish with fresh mint if desired.

Serves 4

Chocolate Souffle (above); Rosehip Pears with Chocolate Sauce (right)

Chocolate Souffle

40 minutes

4 tblspn hot milk

100g (3½oz) dark Club chocolate, melted

1½ tblspn butter

1½ tblspn plain flour

1¼ cup hot milk, extra

½ tspn vanilla essence

4 eggs, separated

4 tblspn castor sugar

icing sugar for dusting

1 Mix the milk into the melted chocolate and set aside.

2 Melt the butter in a medium saucepan over moderate heat, stir in the flour and cook for 30 seconds. Remove from heat, stir in the extra hot milk and vanilla essence, return to the heat and slowly bring to the boil, stirring constantly until sauce thickens.

3 Beat the egg yolks, one at a time, into the chocolate mixture, then beat in the sugar. Beat the egg-whites until soft peaks form. Fold into the chocolate mixture, ½ cup at a time.

4 Grease 4 ¾-cup capacity souffle dishes. Line the top with a collar of greaseproof paper and pour the souffle mixture into the dishes, filling ¾ way up. Bake in moderate oven for 20-25 minutes. Remove the greaseproof paper and dust top with icing sugar. Serve immediately.

Serves 4

Honey Baked Figs

25 minutes

8 fresh figs

2 tblspn brandy

4 tblspn honey

1 Cut figs in half horizontally. Pour ¼ cm (1/8in) water into a baking dish large enough to hold figs in one layer.

2 Arrange figs in the dish, cut side up. Sprinkle each fig with a little brandy. Top figs with 1 teaspoon of honey each.

3 Bake figs in a 220°C (425°F) oven until heated through and bubbly, about 20 minutes. Serve immediately.

Serves 4

Rosehip Pears with Chocolate Sauce

25 minutes

4 ripe, firm pears, peeled

6 rosehip tea bags

4 tblspn butter

¼ cup brown sugar

½ cup sour cream

¼ cup condensed milk

4 tblspn cocoa powder

1 Place pears in a deep saucepan with water to cover, add tea bags and bring water to a simmer. Poach pears until tender, about 20 minutes.

2 Meanwhile, to make sauce: Melt butter in a medium saucepan over moderate heat. Add the sugar, sour cream and condensed milk, stirring constantly, do not boil.

3 Dissolve the cocoa in 3 tblspn water and stir to a paste. Stir into the sauce mixture, bring to a simmer and cook for 1 minute or until sauce thickens.

4 Pour a little sauce into the bottom of each serving glass and place a poached pear in the sauce. Garnish with mint if desired.

Serves 4

Melon and Strawberry Salad with Mint

40 minutes — includes chilling time

1 cantaloupe, cut into bite-size chunks

½ honeydew melon, cut into bite-size chunks

1 punnet strawberries, halved

1 small bunch fresh mint

1 Combine cantaloupe, honeydew and strawberries in a bowl.

2 Roughly chop mint leaves, sprinkle over fruit. Stir gently to mix. Refrigerate for 30 minutes to chill.

3 Divide among 6 dessert plates, serve chilled.

Serves 6

Lime Mousse with Gin

20 minutes

2 large eggs, separated, room temperature

¼ cup sugar

2 tblspn freshly squeezed lime juice

2 tblspn freshly grated lime rind

1 tblspn gin

⅓ cup cream, chilled

1 Beat egg yolks with a hand-held electric mixer together with 2 tablespoons of the sugar until mixture is pale and thick, about 5 minutes.

2 Add lime juice, lime rind and gin, beat a further 3 minutes.

3 In another bowl, beat the egg-whites with a pinch of salt until soft peaks form, gradually add remaining sugar while beating, continue until stiff peaks form. Fold white into the yolk mixture.

4 Beat cream in the egg-white bowl until stiff, fold into egg mixture thoroughly but gently. Spoon mousse into 2 chilled glasses or bowls. Serve immediately.

Serves 2

Pears with Ricotta and Walnuts

10 minutes

375g (¾lb) ricotta cheese

¼ cup cream

¼ cup nut-flavoured liqueur (optional)

¼ cup chopped fresh mint

6 ripe, firm pears, peeled, halved, cored

12 walnut halves, roughly chopped

mint sprigs to garnish

1 In a bowl, combine cheese, cream, liqueur if used, and mint. Beat until smooth.

2 Arrange pears on six dessert plates, top each with a few tablespoons of the cheese mixture. Sprinkle with walnuts, garnish with a sprig of mint. Serve immediately.

Serves 6

Maple Syrup Custards with Poppy Seeds

20 minutes

4 tblspn cream

5 tblspn milk

1 tblspn cornflour

3 tblspn maple syrup

2 tspn poppy seeds, lightly toasted

3 egg yolks

¼ tspn freshly squeezed lemon juice

1 Combine 1 tablespoon of the cream with 2 tablespoons of the milk and the cornflour in a small saucepan. Stir until flour is dissolved, add remaining cream and milk, syrup and poppy seeds, bring to a boil over medium high heat. Remove pan from the heat.

2 In a small bowl, beat egg yolks, whisk in ¼ cup of the hot liquid, whisk egg yolks mixture into the pan. Return pan to a medium heat, stirring constantly, until mixture thickens. Pour into a bowl set over a bowl filled with ice cubes and iced water. Stir until cool.

3 Stir in lemon juice and pour into 2 small souffle dishes. Place under a pre-heated griller until tops are golden brown, about 30 seconds. Serve immediately.

Serves 2

Fruit Salad with Raspberry Sauce

5 minutes

315g (10oz) frozen raspberries, defrosted

2 tblspn castor sugar

1 tblspn freshly squeezed lemon juice

6 cups fresh fruit salad (see note)

1 Place raspberries and their juice in a processor. Add sugar and lemon juice, process until smooth.

2 Divide fruit salad among 6 bowls, pour over sauce. Serve cold.

Note: A number of greengrocers are making their own fresh fruit salad daily.

Serves 6

Zabaglione with Cointreau

15 minutes

9 egg yolks

3 tblspn castor sugar

2 tblspn champagne

4 tblspn Cointreau

1 tblspn grated orange zest

1 cup thickened cream

1 Whisk the egg yolks and sugar in a double saucepan over simmering water until pale yellow, about 5 minutes.

2 Add the champagne, Cointreau, orange zest and cream, and continue to whisk until mixture thickens enough to coat the back of a spoon, about 10 minutes. Serve warm or chilled.

Serves 4

Berry Compote

15 minutes

1 cup boysenberries or blackberries

1 cup raspberries

1 cup fresh strawberries, hulled and halved

¼ cup red wine

3 tblspn freshly squeezed lemon juice

3 tblspn castor sugar

mint to garnish

1 In a small saucepan, heat the berries (excluding strawberries) gently with the red wine, lemon juice and sugar over moderate heat until syrup begins to boil. Remove berries with a slotted spoon and set aside.

2 Boil syrup for 5 minutes.

3 Add the strawberries to the berries and divide between four serving glasses.

4 Cool syrup for 5 minutes, then pour over the berries. Garnish with mint if desired.

Serves 4

Zabaglione with Cointreau (top);
Berry Compote (bottom)

TEMPERATURE AND MEASUREMENT EQUIVALENTS

OVEN TEMPERATURES

	Fahrenheit	Celsius
Very slow	250°	120°
Slow	275–300°	140–150°
Moderately slow	325°	160°
Moderate	350°	180°
Moderately hot	375°	190°
Hot	400–450°	200–230°
Very hot	475–500°	250–260°

CUP AND SPOON MEASURES

Measures given in our recipes refer to the standard metric cup and spoon sets approved by the Standards Association of Australia.

A basic metric cup set consists of 1 cup, ½ cup, ⅓ cup and ¼ cup sizes.

The basic spoon set comprises 1 tablespoon, 1 teaspoon, ½ teaspoon and ¼ teaspoon. These sets are available at leading department, kitchen and hardware stores.

IMPERIAL/METRIC CONVERSION CHART

MASS (WEIGHT)

(Approximate conversions for cookery purposes.)

Imperial	Metric	Imperial	Metric
½ oz	15g	10oz	315g
1oz	30g	11oz	345g
2oz	60g	12oz (¾ lb)	375g
3oz	90g	13oz	410g
4oz (¼ lb)	125g	14oz	440g
5oz	155g	15oz	470g
6oz	185g	16oz (1lb)	500g (0.5kg)
7oz	220g	24oz (1½ lb)	750g
8oz (½ lb)	250g	32oz (2lb)	1000g (1kg)
9oz	280g	3lb	1500g (1.5kg)

METRIC CUP AND SPOON SIZES

Cup	Spoon
¼ cup = 60ml	¼ teaspoon = 1.25ml
⅓ cup = 80ml	½ teaspoon = 2.5ml
½ cup = 125ml	1 teaspoon = 5ml
1 cup = 250ml	1 tablespoon = 20ml

LIQUIDS

Imperial	Cup*	Metric
1fl oz		30ml
2fl oz	¼ cup	60ml
3fl oz		100ml
4fl oz	½ cup	125ml

LIQUIDS (cont'd)

Imperial	Cup*	Metric
5fl oz (¼ pint)		150ml
6fl oz	¾ cup	200ml
8fl oz	1 cup	250ml
10fl oz (½ pint)	1¼ cups	300ml
12fl oz	1½ cups	375ml
14fl oz	1¾ cups	425ml
15fl oz		475ml
16fl oz	2 cups	500ml
20fl oz (1 pint)	2½ cups	600ml

* Cup measures are the same in Imperial and Metric.

LENGTH

Inches	Centimetres	Inches	Centimetres
¼	0.5	7	18
½	1	8	20
¾	2	9	23
1	2.5	10	25
1½	4	12	30
2	5	14	35
2½	6	16	40
3	8	18	45
4	10	20	50
6	15		

NB: 1cm = 10mm.